TAKING AIM AT THE
PRESIDENT

TAKING AIM AT THE
PRESIDENT

THE REMARKABLE STORY OF THE WOMAN
WHO SHOT AT GERALD FORD

GERI SPIELER

palgrave
macmillan

First published in 2009 by PALGRAVE MACMILLAN® in the
United States—a division of St. Martin's Press LLC, 175 Fifth Avenue,
New York, NY 10010.

Where this book is distributed in the UK, Europe and the rest of the
world, this is by Palgrave Macmillan, a division of Macmillan
Publishers Limited, registered in England, company number 785998,
of Houndmills, Basingstoke, Hampshire RG21 6XS.

Palgrave Macmillan is the global academic imprint of the above
companies and has companies and representatives throughout the
world.

Palgrave® and Macmillan® are registered trademarks in the United
States, the United Kingdom, Europe and other countries.

ISBN-13: 978-0-230-61023-1
ISBN-10: 0-230-61023-4

Library of Congress Cataloging-in-Publication Data
Spieler, Geri.
   Taking aim at the president : the remarkable story of the woman
who shot at Gerald Ford / Geri Spieler.
      p.   cm.
   ISBN 0-230-61023-4
   1. Moore, Sara Jane, 1940–   2. Ford, Gerald R., 1913–2006—
Assassination attempt, 1975 (September 22)   3. Assassins—United
States—Biography.   4. Housewives—United States—Biography.
5. Charleston (W. Va.)—Biography.   I. Title.
E866.3.S68   2009
364.152'4092—dc22
[B]

                                                        2008024812

A catalogue record of the book is available from the British Library.

Design by Letra Libre, Inc.

First edition: January 2009
10 9 8 7 6 5 4 3 2 1
Printed in the United States of America.

To my loving husband, Rick Kaplowitz

CONTENTS

Photosection appears between pages 128–129.

ACKNOWLEDGMENTS

"Energy and Persistence conquer all things."
—*Benjamin Franklin*

While Franklin's adage may be true, often a cast of characters is present that provides love, patience, excellent advice, and endless enthusiasm.

A project of this kind involves many, many people. I owe a great debt to those who generously shared the intimate details of their lives with me so that I could reconstruct the human experience of these events beyond the newspaper headlines. Many of the key sources of this information must remain anonymous; I honor their trust. My deepest gratitude goes to those who provided information and guided me to others who shared critical details. Without them, this book could not have been completed.

My husband, Rick Kaplowitz, is the most patient, supportive, wise, and knowledgeable person I have ever had the good fortune to know and love. Without his encouragement, guidance, and endless hours of help—in matters large and small—this experience would not have been as rich—or as much fun.

My agent, Sharlene Martin, the most tenacious person I know, is my cheerleader, my psychologist, a friend, and the tiger in my corner. Many thanks to editor Naomi Luchs Seigel, for her herculean support and broad shoulders.

Enormous thanks go to my Palgrave Macmillan editor, Alessandra Bastagli, who wins first prize for her brilliance, talent, and, most of all, patience and understanding. Thank you, Alessandra, for your wonderful insight and challenging questions. You made it work.

How can I possibly thank those of Sara Jane's children and surviving siblings who agreed to speak with me, providing critical details for this work? Their generosity of spirit, trust, time, and energy cannot be measured and their contributions have ensured the book's authenticity.

I also had the good fortune to connect with many other people in Sara Jane's life: former classmates, neighbors, law enforcement officers, and others who came in either close or casual contact with my subject. My deepest gratitude to Irene McCollam, who provided many, many contacts for me (Irene stealthily arranged entry to Sara Jane's high school reunion), and one of Sara Jane's neighbors, Bob Turkelson, who provided important details of her early years.

To my writers circle and fellow members of the San Francisco/Peninsula Branch of the California Writers Club, particularly Ann Foster, Mary Hanna, Tory Hartmann, Dale King, Elliotte Mao, Bree La Maire, and Linda Okerlund for your support and many hours chasing errors.

I also want to thank the librarians in Charleston, West Virginia, for many hours of assistance in providing the details of life in Charleston and access to their collection *Infamous West Virginians*.

TAKING AIM AT THE
PRESIDENT

PROLOGUE

*There comes a point when the only way you can
make a statement is to pick up a gun.*

—Sara Jane Moore[1]

In September 1975, when I saw the photos of Sara Jane Moore being driven off to jail after her attempt on the life of President Gerald R. Ford, like so many others, I found the idea that this snub-nosed, apple-cheeked, middle-class mom had fired a weapon at the president almost impossible to believe.

At age forty-five, Sara Jane Moore was several years older than I was at the time, but we had one thing in common: We both had young sons. I pictured my child, alone in the world as his mother was carted off to a federal prison, and my heart immediately went out to this little boy.

On October 15, 1975, I received a handwritten note from Sara Jane, inviting me to visit her. The note was sent to me in care of the *Los Angeles News Journal*, where I worked. She had read an article I had written about a class-action suit against Sybil Brand Institute, Los Angeles County's women's jail,[2] and she thought I would be a sympathetic ear. Further, she would begin serving her sentence at the Federal Correctional Institution at Terminal Island in San Pedro, California, just five miles from where I lived with my husband and young son. I was intrigued.

As the day for my visit approached, I tried to imagine what she would be like. It was January 1976. I couldn't wait to meet the woman who had attempted to assassinate a U.S. president, a woman the newspapers described as sharp-tongued, scatter-brained, uncommunicative, and uncooperative. But the woman who approached me at the prison was not like that at all. She entered the room with confidence, extending her hand to me with a warm and friendly gesture. She was middle-aged, of medium height, blue-eyed, with short, curly brown hair. She could easily have been my neighbor. She looked me straight in the eye with a clear gaze.

"I'm so glad you came," she said, smiling broadly.

The disconnect was stunning. She behaved as if we were meet-ing for lunch at Chez Panisse, a five star restaurant in Berkeley, rather than sitting in the middle of a human storage facility. "By the way," she asked with interest, "how old did you say your son is?" I had to stop her right then and there. I could sense that she was trying to smooth-talk me. Maybe I never tried to murder any-one, but I did grow up in Los Angeles and I wasn't totally without some street savvy.

"Listen, Sara Jane," I began.

She jumped in, "Oh, call me Sally. All my friends call me Sally."

"OK, Sally, Sara Jane, look, I did not come here because I'm a fan of yours. I also didn't come here to save you and I'm certainly no sympathizer. I think what you tried to do was very wrong. I came because I'm a journalist and you asked me to come. I told you in my letter I'm not assigned to write about you. So, what is it you wanted to talk to me about?"

She ignored my speech and went on to tell me that she needed help getting birthday and Christmas gifts to her son. She asked if I could help with that.

This was the quintessential Sara Jane, the persona she presented to the world. But this was not the only Sara Jane I came to know over the next thirty years. She might have been sitting in prison, but prison would only be a backdrop for her many personas: the gracious hostess, the efficient manager, the homey and talented seamstress and handicrafter, the valiant fighter for justice, or whoever she decided she would display to the world. That day, she was the gracious hostess. This was her reality; and like so many others in her life, I often took it at face value for many years. It took me far too long to understand that her reality generally wasn't the one most of us inhabit.

I would also eventually discover that Sara Jane was charming and gracious when she wanted to be. For a long time she got a lot of support from me in multiple ways—I served as a sounding board, as someone to send gifts to her son on her behalf and to send clothes to her during the years when the inmates were allowed to wear street garments. Once a year she would also receive a gift box, which usually contained toiletries, as long as I had it sent directly from a business.

I was happy to provide her with other conveniences, such as reading material. I knew that the women in the facility were always hungry for good reading because the bookmobile, a mobile library, had a limited selection, and that books were shared widely in the population. And, during those times when I could afford it, I sent her a small monthly allowance.

On my visits Sara Jane would "perform" and talk as if she were still entertaining in her suburban home in Danville, California, thirty miles from the city by the Bay.

Her letters to me were all very similar: perfectly printed, grammatically flawless, and excruciatingly detailed. They usually began with a "Thank you for . . ." and she always remembered to ask about my son and to highlight the similarities in our lives. No challenges, no questions, just polite and newsy letters and phone calls.

I never had a reason to doubt what she told me, and I never questioned her or checked on anything she said. It didn't matter, and I just assumed that what she said was true. After all, why would she lie to me?

In 2003, my schedule became more flexible and I went to see Sara Jane. It had been more than a year since my last visit.

When I explained that I had some time on my hands, Sara Jane said, "Well, now you should get back to your real writing."

"What do you suggest I write about?"

"Maybe it is finally time to write my book."

We talked about what it would mean for me to transition from a regular visitor to an official journalist, with privileges to bring in a tape recorder and paper for notes—more than just a plastic sandwich bag full of change for the vending machines.

As I began to sketch out a schedule and create lists of people, Sara Jane started canceling our visits. She would call me at the last minute, on the same morning I was to drive seventy minutes to reach the latest prison relocation. Breathless, she would tell me on the phone that some prison issue had suddenly come up and I couldn't get in to see her.

On our last visit, I began to gently ask her about growing up in Charleston, West Virginia. Her back stiffened and her head twisted in my direction.

"How did you know that I was from Charleston? I never told you where I grew up."

"I know you didn't tell me. You didn't have to. It was all over every news story ever written about you," I said.

Through clenched teeth, she replied, "That may be. But *I* didn't tell you."

This exchange raised one of several small red flags. Sara Jane's demand for control was going to be a problem.

I had put out requests for interviews to many people who could tell me about Sara Jane's early life. One such person was Father Bill O'Donnell, a Catholic priest at St. Joseph the Worker Church in Berkeley. Sara Jane had first met him when they both attended a rally in support of the Delano grape strike that focused on migrant workers' rights and was led by César Chávez in the late 1960s. They had maintained contact into the seventies, and Father Bill had been there to counsel Sara Jane after she was arrested in 1975.

Being the honorable man that he was, Father Bill wrote to Sara Jane about my request for an interview. On an August evening in 2003, Sara Jane called me at home. At first she was calm, but I could hear the tension in her voice. Gradually her voice rose in anger: "How dare you ask to talk to Father Bill!"

She did not like that I was doing research about the book without her direct and detailed involvement. I told her that since it had been increasingly difficult to visit and speak with her, I had figured I might move forward more rapidly by interviewing people she knew.

She proceeded to tell me exactly how this project was going to be done: she would approve my book proposal to be sure it was the book she wanted to publish; she would supply me with a list of interviewees; and she would read and approve everything I wrote. Then she demanded to see and review my contract with my agent, and said she would call her after that review.

My response was simple. "That is not how I work," I explained to her. "If I am going to write your book, you must give me some room. And, you need to cooperate with me. You need to talk with me about your life. Your *entire* life."

I waited through a few uneasy minutes of silence as she pondered how to phrase her response. After one more very audible breath, and with great intensity, she clearly enunciated each word: "I am no longer at home to you." Then she slammed down the receiver.

That was the last time Sara Jane Moore and I spoke to each other. She never participated in the active writing of this book, but

I had twenty-eight years of conversations and letters prior to that date that I could refer to.

When I began to research the life of the woman who was Sara Jane Kahn, I began to uncover information that led me to believe there was much more to her story than I'd ever heard from her directly. I also ran into many false leads and dead ends, which made me even more determined to find out the story behind this woman I thought I knew.

I faced many challenges while researching Sara Jane's life—from her habit of distorting and withholding information as she pleased, to the fact that key documentation covering large swaths of her life was either unavailable or destroyed, and many details were impossible to corroborate. This obliged me, at times, to leave gaps in the narrative, and I have pointed these out in the text as they occur. Although the research process was frustrating at times, I always believed that Sara Jane's is an important story to tell.

My search eventually led me to a hilltop home in Charleston, West Virginia, where Sara Jane grew up. Her story must begin there.

ONE

THE GIRL WHO DISAPPEARED

In the days immediately following Sara Jane Moore's attempt to assassinate President Gerald R. Ford on September 22, 1975, the press scrambled to find any information at all about this woman who had appeared out of nowhere. Both the *San Francisco Chronicle* and the *New York Times* ran front page stories the next day, describing her as stemming from an impoverished neighborhood in Charleston, West Virginia. The accounts also repeated Sara Jane's claim, told to one of the police officers detaining her, that she was descended from a West Virginia oil and timber baron. Neither description was accurate. In fact, the only correct information about her early background in either account was the identity of her home state, West Virginia, where she was born Sara Jane Kahn, the second daughter of Olaf and Ruth Kahn, on February 15, 1930.

At a glance the Kahns presented a picture-perfect image of a twentieth-century middle-class American family: three brothers, two sisters, and their parents lived in the hilltop house at the north edge of Charleston, West Virginia, nestled in the lush Appalachian Mountains and overlooking the Kanawha River. The neighbors immediately to the south of the Kahn house were set on ten acres and had six milk cows; they used part of their land for pasture, and part was planted with corn, beans, tomatoes, and several acres of green onions. Several other small farms were also nearby. The semi-rural neighborhood, a community of several hundred homes, had a small-town feel, and it was built around family and the local schools. Neighbors were close by and they often observed birthdays and holidays at home with family and friends. It was a perfect neighborhood for children. The five Kahn children had plenty of room to run and play.

Home was a two-story log structure with covered porches running the length of the house, set on five sloping acres. A thicket of woods reached right up to the back of the house. In the long daylight hours of the summer season and on weekends well into the fall, the Kahn family would tend their vegetable garden. Ruth canned tomatoes, as well as applesauce, peaches, and pears. Eggs gathered from their chickens, and sometimes the chickens themselves, fed the family; the Kahns also sold chickens and eggs as a supplemental source of income. The house had two stone fireplaces, one in the living room and one in the parlor. Although each fireplace was sixty inches long and thirty inches deep, Olaf—mindful of the hard times of the 1930s—built a gas heater into each fireplace, knowing the family would get more economical and efficient heat that way.

Olaf Kahn had grown up on a small rural farm in Flatbrookville, in eastern New Jersey, where his parents had moved after emigrating from Germany just before the turn of the century. He became a U.S. marine in 1917 after graduating from high school and served in France during World War I. Like his future wife, Ruth, Olaf was an accomplished violinist, until he injured his right hand in the service. His hand healed, but his days as a violinist were over. Following his injury, the Marines sent Olaf to

Charleston, West Virginia, as part of a group sent to help clean up a chlorine spill. While serving on that detail, Olaf began to interact with engineers at the DuPont plant, and he was quickly recognized for his contributions to their work.

He settled in Charleston when he was mustered out of the service, and was immediately hired to work as a mechanical engineer by DuPont. Olaf would eventually become superintendent at the Belle plant site, eight miles east of Charleston on the Kanawha River. A trim six feet tall with sandy hair, high cheekbones, and a pleasant face, Olaf earned an annual salary of $10,000, a very respectable income during the Great Depression.

Ruth Moore Kahn was ten years younger than her husband. She stood about five feet two inches tall and had curly red hair. Ruth was a violinist with the Charleston Symphony Orchestra, and music was one of the special bonds that she and Olaf shared. She was just twenty years old and newly married when her first daughter, Ruth Ann, was born. Sara Jane arrived three years later. Olaf II came along in 1932 and was nicknamed Skippy early on. Another son, Paul, was born in 1935, but survived for only five days before succumbing to lung congestion and other developmental disabilities. Ruth became pregnant again just over a year later, and son Dana joined the family in 1937. Charles, the youngest, was born in 1941.

Ruth Kahn was more vivacious than the solid and dependable Olaf, but she too was a hard worker, forever cleaning and picking up after the kids; she kept the Kahn home white-glove clean. She dressed her daughters in the latest fashions, from their Shirley Temple hairdos to their patent leather shoes. She was an expert seamstress, and made many of their dresses herself without commercial patterns—right down to impeccably smocked bodices. A former neighbor said Ruth Kahn could "smock a dress like nobody's business" for her own or a neighbor's daughter, and she knew at least eight different smocking stitches.

"She was known as the neighborhood mom," recalled Bob Turkelson, a neighbor of Sara Jane's, in a personal interview. "Ruth was the person to go to if you had a problem, no matter who you were."

Bob shared a story about a time he came home from school to find his mother was not at home and the family doctor was waiting for him. The doctor took ten-year-old Bob by the hand and walked him up the street to the Kahn's house. When they went inside, Bob saw his mother collapsed in the arms of Ruth Kahn, crying. Bob's older brother had died in an automobile accident.

Ruth loved her family and worked hard to turn the holidays into festive occasions, not only for her own children, but for the neighbors' kids, too. At Halloween she carved pumpkins and set up an elaborate horror house designed to scare and delight the children—complete with spooky noises, cobwebs, and peeled grapes as eyes for the blindfolded guests to touch. She was famous in the neighborhood for baking birthday cakes with buttercream frosting. This was unusual during the Depression because of the scarcity of many food items, but somehow Ruth Kahn always had plenty of butter, milk, eggs, and sugar for a birthday cake. Neighbors and friends of the Kahn children never missed one of their birthday parties.

Ruth's earnings from the symphony orchestra and the chicken-and-egg money supplemented Olaf's salary. All of the children took music and dance lessons; every family member played at least one instrument. Ruth Ann, a bright girl who grew into a tall young woman with an ethereal look, played the flute. Sara Jane played the violin, although she frequently complained about the drudgery of practicing. Often, the family would gather with their instruments, accompanied by Olaf at the old upright piano.

Mornings in the Kahn household were hectic as adults and kids poured out of the four upstairs bedrooms. In the afternoons, one or two of the kids were always at Ruth's kitchen table, doing homework or snacking before chores. In the evenings, the family would gather for dinner, and Olaf demanded that the children behave during the meal. After dinner, the kids cleared the table and then worked on homework or practiced their instruments. As Ruth fussed in the kitchen, Olaf would remove his suit jacket and settle into his upholstered easy chair in the living room. The radio console played classical music softly in the background, and a lit cigarette dangled between his long fingers as he read the *Charleston Daily Mail*. Skip told me that he rarely saw his father dressed in anything but a three-piece suit.

"Every morning, at breakfast and at dinner, my father was dressed properly in one of his three-piece suits, his shirts perfectly starched," Skip said. He recalled that the only times his father did not wear a suit were the rare occasions when he went out in the field to sow corn.

A closer look at this idyllic picture of the Kahn family reveals some cracks. Ruth was a solid neighborhood mom, but she was also a perfectionist; she was rarely satisfied with her children's efforts. She held herself and her children to very high standards; when Ruth Ann or Sara Jane finished a chore, Ruth would inspect their work. More often than not, she'd declare the job not good enough and redo it herself.

Olaf, too, had very strict limits and a cutting tongue that could slice through his children's self-confidence. His after-dinner ritual, for example, was not to be interrupted for any reason. In the rare instance when a child actually summoned the courage to walk into the living room to ask a question about a homework assignment, Olaf's response was cold. Raising his eyebrows, he would fix one eye on the child and stare through the curling smoke of his cigarette. In a firm, flat monotone, he would say, "If I told you, you wouldn't understand anyway." Most of the children never made that mistake twice, son Skip said.[1] Olaf was an old-fashioned patriarch who kept his personal struggles to himself.

Further examination of the Kahn family would also reveal that at least one member of the family did not seem to fit in. Early photos of Sara Jane show a slight girl with shoulder-length brown hair, sad blue eyes, and a delicate but impenetrable air. In the midst of her family, Sara Jane stood just outside the circle of brothers and sisters. Ruth Ann, two years older, was formidable in her religious devotion. She found her escape immediately after college by marrying a minister and never moving back home. The three boys, Skip, Dana, and Charles, formed a boisterous familial bond as teenagers. High school sports defined the relationships among the boys both at home and with their many friends. In their routine there was no room for sisters.

Sara Jane excelled academically. She was bright and curious, a straight "A" student (she even skipped a grade in elementary school), an accomplished violinist, a ballet student, an excellent seamstress like her mother, and a talented actor and artist. Yet something was clearly amiss, and most people who came into contact with her sensed it. One of Sara Jane's junior high school teachers delicately described her as "a little odd." The oddity was her lack of connectedness with her teachers and other students. She isolated herself from them and found escape and satisfaction in acting class, submerging herself in different roles. A ballet-school classmate recalled that at age thirteen, "She was always making up something bizarre. She would come in and tell the craziest stories about her family being descendents of royalty."

Neighbors from Woodward Drive and her classmates from Stonewall Jackson High remember Sara Jane as "aloof" but "intense," "unfriendly" but "looking for the limelight"—and, always, "a little odd." Adults in the neighborhood tried hard to make sure the other children did not exclude her. "Be nice to Sara Jane, even though she seems hard to get to know," her Girl Scout troop leader instructed the other girls more than once. But it didn't help, a troop member said. "Even if you were nice to her, she never reciprocated. She never tried to really be a part of anything, even when we tried to bring her in. She never had any friends."

Paradoxically, Sara Jane often demanded that she be the center of attention no matter how uncomfortable that might make others. One former neighbor remembered attending Sara Jane's thirteenth birthday party; Ruth had invited the neighborhood kids. They may not have been fond of Sara Jane, but the promise of one of Ruth's delicious cakes probably clinched the deal for most of them. When the kids arrived at the party, however, Sara Jane insisted that they all had to sit and listen to her perform a violin recital before the cake was served.

Sara Jane found a new way to capture the limelight at Charleston's Stonewall Jackson High School, where her studies began in 1944. She had joined Thespians, the drama club. Although she was still not sought after as a friend, she was respected as an actor and was considered intensely dedicated to the art. Early on, it was clear that Sara Jane was adept at role-playing. She auditioned for the lead in every new production and won roles in several plays, including *Why the Chimes Rang* and *The Late Christopher Bean*. As one of her classmates told me, "It seemed as though she was clearly headed for an acting career."

She also joined the Spanish club, where she soon acquired a reputation as a fluent Spanish speaker. According to a fellow Spanish club member, Sara Jane was "studying Spanish as though she were going to Spain."

Sara Jane did nothing at half speed. She prided herself in being an excellent student, and found no academic challenge too difficult or intimidating. She had such confidence in her intellect that she felt nothing she attempted was unachievable. Her school report on *Ivanhoe* was expertly prepared. She labored over the manuscript for hours, carefully hand-printing the text as through it were typeset and adding beautifully executed drawings. Her violin playing approached concert quality.

The centrally located Diamond Department Store, downtown at Capital and Washington Streets, was the social extension of several generations of Charleston students. They flowed into the store's coffee, Coke, and sandwich shop after school and on Saturdays to hang out. Young girls sat on high stools at the wide marble counter of the soda fountain, legs crossed demurely, giggling with their friends. Couples going steady snuggled close at the small round wire-legged tables, drinking from a single soda with two straws. On Friday and Saturday nights, boys slouched outside the front door while girls walked down the street with their friends, flirting and pretending to ignore them. It was an American ritual.

But Sara Jane was not to be found with the other teens at the Diamond. Her interactions were reserved for responding eagerly to teachers' questions. Instead of flirting with the boys or laughing with her girlfriends, she moved purposefully from class to class, a stack of books in her arms and a very serious expression on her face. Her arena for social acceptance was limited to clubs focused on a goal. If she could not compete socially, then she would compete academically. Sara, her brother Skip said, was very proud of her academic achievements.

Along with many teens, women, and men who were too old for the armed services, Sara Jane spent the final years of World War II as an active member of Charleston's Civil Air Patrol (CAP).[2] The CAP, an organization that began as a volunteer force of civilian pilots in World War II patrolling the American coastline and bombing German U-boats, encouraged students to learn about aviation, weapons, and leadership in a military setting. One of the few girls in the CAP, Sara Jane excelled in the program. She was quick to learn the instruments when the group was taken on an orientation flight in a Cessna 310. She may also have had some initial familiarization with weapons. Sara Jane wore her uniform with pride.

Her family and friends assumed that Sara Jane was headed for some sort of conventional career—perhaps as an actress or a Spanish teacher or a musician. Perhaps, despite her social awkwardness, she would fall in love and start a family. Then, she began what would turn into a lifelong pattern: She disappeared.

One day in the fall of 1946, when Sara Jane was sixteen, she left home for school but never showed up. That evening she didn't return home. She hadn't left a note, and she hadn't mentioned to anyone that she was going anywhere. Her parents were frantic. Her schoolmates were questioned, along with teachers, drama tutors, and members of the Spanish club and of the CAP. No one knew of any school-related activities or of possible relationships that would have called her away.

Ruth and Olaf mounted a full search, but they could find no sign of their daughter. Finally, they reported her disappearance to the police. The police could find no trace of her. Three days later, just as suddenly as she had disappeared, Sara Jane returned. She looked exactly as she had when she left for school. Where had she been? She offered no explanation. She refused to talk to anyone about it. Ruth, thinking she might have been abducted and sexually assaulted, had her daughter examined by the family doctor, who reported no signs of "abuse." Sara Jane was not injured, did not appear traumatized, and apparently had not been kidnapped. Eventually, Ruth chose to explain her child's disappearance as "amnesia," and left it at that. Sara Jane remained silent.

Sara Jane resumed her life at school without a word of explanation. Then, in a sudden show of independence, Sara Jane announced that she would get a job so she could have her own money to do with as she pleased. Her brother Skip had a morning paper route, delivering the *Charleston Daily Mail*. Sara Jane secured the delivery job for the afternoon paper, the *Charleston Gazette*.

"I think Sara was the only girl I knew with a paper route," her brother Skip told me. "She always liked to do things her own way."

Once she made a decision, Sara Jane was steadfast in her position. On a Sunday morning, as the family prepared to go to the

Baptist church, Sara Jane announced she would attend the Methodist church instead.

Skip said it would do no good to argue with his sister. "If she had a belief in something, she pursued it. Whatever Sara became interested in she would research it. She could always back up her beliefs."

Upon graduation in 1947, Sara stayed at home and decided to pursue a career in medicine, which, at a time when few women even contemplated becoming doctors, meant becoming a nurse. She was easily admitted to Charleston's St. Francis Hospital School of Nursing, where she soon earned a record as a top-notch student nurse. The nursing school administrators gave her glowing reports. Of course, nothing less than perfection was acceptable to young Sara Jane Kahn. However, as soon as she got within arm's reach of the brass ring, she drew back and went in search of something else.

At the end of a semester in nursing school, instead of signing up for classes for the following term, she abruptly dropped out and joined the Women's Army Corps (WAC). The WAC was formed by Congress in 1942 to allow women to enter the military in noncombat positions. Her parents were puzzled by this sudden change of heart, but Sara Jane gave no explanation.

When Sara joined, service in the WAC consisted of relieving thousands of men of their clerical assignments. The WAC women performed jobs such as radio operator, electrician, and air traffic controller. After the war, the army continued to use these women to staff army hospitals and administrative centers.

After basic training, Private First Class Sara Kahn was assigned to a unit in the Carlisle Barracks in Pennsylvania, and she left Charleston forever. She had traded in her starched white nurse's uniform for military khakis, and a brand-new persona appeared. Sara Jane, striving as always for maximum achievement, told her family that her goal was to qualify for Officers Candidate

School (OCS). After scoring top grades on the written qualifying test and performing all military details—including firearms training—with excellence, she was duly selected for OCS.[3]

Attending OCS was Sara Jane's opportunity to become a commissioned officer in the WAC. She would have gone to Fort Benning, Georgia, for training that started with an initial twelve-week session to evaluate leadership strengths. Upon graduation from the training, she would have become a second lieutenant.

Almost immediately, however, she embarked on two ventures that ensured she would never be an officer. The first was the building of a record at the Carlisle Barracks of what the military described as a recurring series of fainting spells. The second was her marriage to Marine Staff Sergeant Wallace E. Anderson, a noncommissioned officer at Carlisle. Sara Jane married him in spite of the fact that marriage would bar her from OCS.

The fainting spells culminated on a beautiful spring day in 1950. The National Mall in Washington, D.C. was aglow with cherry blossoms. Twenty-year-old Sara Jane, alone and out of uniform in a neatly tailored light pastel spring suit, had joined a public tour of the accessible part of the White House. At the end of the tour, she walked slowly away from the tour group and across the White House lawn—and dropped to the ground, apparently in a dead faint. Bystanders and Secret Service agents rushed to her assistance. When she regained consciousness, she claimed not to know who or where she was. Finding no identification papers of any kind on her person, the Secret Service agents took her to Walter Reed Army Hospital for assessment. As the nurses there undressed her for bed, they discovered something odd: a small folio of photos stuffed up under the bodice of her dress. All the pictures were of Sara Jane.

The newspapers published several of her photographs, alongside inquiries as to whether anyone could identify her.[4] They didn't have to wait long: Her mother in Charleston and her husband in Pennsylvania both saw the photos and rushed to Sara Jane's hospital bedside to identify her. Her memory soon returned, but the FBI was suspicious. Their investigation concluded that Sara Jane had purposely left all of her identification behind.

TWO

THE UNHAPPY HOUSEWIFE

Soon after the fainting incident, Sara Jane made two changes in her life: She divorced her Marine Corps husband, Wally Anderson, and she left the WACs. Only a few months later, in November 1950, Sara Jane married another military man—Sydney Lewis Manning, an air force captain. Syd, a career officer originally from Los Angeles and some seventeen years older than Sara Jane, had worked his way up through the ranks. He had served twenty years in the air force, having joined up right out of high school, and planned to retire from the service in 1951, still a relatively young man. But his half pension would not have stretched far enough to support Sara Jane and the family they planned to have, so Syd returned to active duty. The couple was billeted to Davis-Monthan Air Force Base adjacent to Tucson, Arizona.

World War II was six years in the past, and the Cold War was in its first phase. Earlier that same year, Senator Joseph McCarthy had asserted that Communist spies had infiltrated the U.S. State

Department, perhaps at the highest levels. The American celebration that had followed the end of World War II had been quickly replaced by a pervasive feeling of unease and the suspicion that Communists were hiding under every bed. The 43rd Air Refueling Squadron, headquartered at Davis-Monthan, stood ready to defend the nation if called upon.

All Sara Jane wanted now was to pursue her interests without interference out west in Arizona with her flyboy husband. Instead, she ended up in the drab, cookie-cutter housing projects provided by the air force. The only difference from one house to the next was the shade of green paint—slightly lighter or darker. Sara Jane, being her mother's daughter, would have wasted no time in using her creativity to make her home stand out from all the others and reflect her personal sense of style.

Most days, she would have been left to fend for herself while Syd went on extended temporary duty assignments away from Arizona. The lives of air force wives revolved around house visits for coffee and cards, with a special fuss made whenever one of them became pregnant. Sara Jane would likely have received such attention when she became pregnant with her first child. Sydney Jr. was born in 1951.[1] When Ruth, Olaf, and Sara's brother Charles visited Sara Jane and the baby during the holidays that year, they immediately saw that the young mother was overwhelmed by the task of maintaining feeding schedules and keeping Sydney Jr. clean and neat. Ever the perfectionist, Ruth was particularly critical of Sara Jane's efforts to manage the house and the baby. To Ruth, no house was ever as clean as she thought it should be, and Sara Jane was just not cutting it. Skip, her oldest brother, remembered his mother's distress after the visit. To her way of thinking, the baby was never changed fast enough, laundry was not done often enough, and dinners were not timely enough. Sara Jane was a dismal failure as a housewife, according to her mother's standards.

By Christmas 1952 Sara Jane was already expecting her second child. It looked like she might well be on her way to a life as a stay-at-home mother and homemaker. However, she must have been deeply uncomfortable with that lifestyle, with groups of what she surely deemed to be superficial women gathering to gossip and watch their children play. The early 1950s were a relatively apolitical era of disinterest in idealistic causes. Recovering from World War II, people were serene and uninvolved; there was little attention to or concern for social issues. The nation at large accepted without question the traditional American values of work, order, and patriotism.[2]

When her daughter Janet was born in 1953, Sara Jane was confirmed in the one role that she was not prepared for: full-time motherhood. To her, the 1950s Ozzie and Harriet role model of the stay-at-home mom in high heels, apron permanently tied with a bow, and complete contentment as the happy housekeeper seemed more like homemaker hell. With each addition to the family, Sara Jane and Syd grew further apart; eventually they barely spoke. Syd accepted more overseas assignments and saw little of his children.

Ruth called Sara Jane daily and became more distressed with each conversation. She concluded that her daughter was becoming increasingly dysfunctional as a wife and mother. She took comfort in the fact that Sara Jane was not neglecting her children outright, but she worried that her daughter did not take any joy in them either. Sara Jane, as a wife and mother, did what she thought she should do, all the while resenting her role.

When Syd was home, his interactions with Sara Jane grew increasingly unpleasant. He could no longer tolerate his wife's behavior and filed for divorce. His reasons included accusations that she was an extremely poor mother and wife. On October 7, 1954, Syd and Sara Jane's divorce became official. Almost immediately, however, he had second thoughts; he missed his family, and the couple reconciled and remarried in November of the same year. Syd was soon reassigned to Los Angeles, and the reconnected family moved to southern California, where Syd had been raised. His home town was Cardiff, located fifty miles north of San Diego.

Once Sara Jane was settled in, despite having to care for two toddlers, she somehow managed to meet and mingle with a small circle of Hollywood actors and directors. How she met these people is unclear, but she attended several Hollywood parties while her husband was away on military duty.

While Sara Jane was pregnant with her third child, she had an unannounced visitor. On a warm day late in the spring of 1954, Sara Jane answered a knock at her apartment door. A tall, handsome air force lieutenant whom she didn't recognize stood in front of her. At first, she thought he was a friend of her husband's, but then she saw a funny and somewhat familiar grin on his face.

"Hey, Sis, don't you know your own brother?" It was Skip, stopping by for a surprise visit, hoping to meet Syd and the kids.

After two days he had a pretty good picture of Sara Jane's life. She seemed to be taking care of the family, Skip told me. Sydney Jr. and Janet were clean and neat; but Sara Jane seemed distant from them. "There was just something odd, but I couldn't tell you exactly what it was."

"I do know she was sewing a lot," Skip said. "It is something I'll just never forget. It was as though she had got a great bargain on a bolt of blue gingham. Her entire apartment was a vision in blue gingham: Sara Jane had sewn curtains, tablecloths, napkins, a maternity dress, an apron, and little Sydney's sun suit all out of the same material."

Melissa was born in Los Angeles on October 30, 1954, and was severely disabled from birth. She was institutionalized directly from the hospital, and was eventually taken in and raised by a family that offered foster care to mentally handicapped children.

Sara Jane let her mother handle all the details regarding her infant daughter, and once Melissa was tucked away in an institution, Sara Jane dismissed her from her life. According to Skip, Ruth took on the responsibility of checking regularly on Melissa's welfare.

Ruth, meanwhile, was enjoying her middle years. With most of her children grown and out of the house, she was spending more and more time on her church work. But she was losing sleep about Sara Jane and the grandchildren because of what she had heard from Skip.

Her observations during her earlier visit had both puzzled and frightened her: Sara Jane was an indifferent and irresponsible mother. She was not paying enough attention to her young children, and that was cause for concern. So, in the spring of 1955, Ruth flew out to Los Angeles to see if she could provide some hands-on help. When she arrived, things were worse than she had imagined. Sara Jane was clearly not coping very well, and was certainly not fulfilled by motherhood. In fact, *nothing* seemed to be working: The kids were fed on an erratic schedule, and the chaotic household never settled into the warmth of a home. During her ten-day visit, Ruth simply took over and ran things, cleaning the house, cooking, and ensuring that the children had proper meals at regular times. Sara Jane was frustrated about being in Los Angeles saddled with two young children and a mostly absent husband. This life had none of the allure of nearby Hollywood and the acting career her Stonewall classmates had thought was her destiny. So when Ruth offered to take the two children back to Charleston for a visit that summer, Sara Jane quickly and gratefully accepted.

Sydney Jr. and Janet flew back with Ruth to West Virginia. They spent a month and a half with the members of the Kahn family, all of whom did their best to help Ruth. Brothers Dana and Charles, still at home, would frequently take one or both of the children out to play. They went on park outings, story sessions at the library, visits to the zoo, and occasionally a children's movie matinee. Everyone hoped that giving Sara Jane a chance to rest up and have some time to herself would recharge her batteries and re-build the energy she needed to be a better mother.

Finally, the two children returned to California. The atmosphere at "home" with their mother was very different from the love and warmth they had found with their aunts, uncles, cousins, and grandparents in West Virginia.

Sara Jane and Syd's second marriage lasted little more than a year. This time, in October 1955, it was Sara Jane—pregnant again—who filed for divorce, claiming irreconcilable differences.

Christopher, soon nicknamed Chris, was born in 1955.[3] Sara Jane was now alone in Los Angeles with three children under the age of six. As most people would be under the circumstances, she was likely tired, unable to remember the last time she had slept through the night. There would have been incessant demands on her, day in and day out, and never any relief from the chores and the noise and the diapers and the shopping and the feedings and the laundry. This could not have been what Sara Jane had envisioned for her life, and apparently she was finding it increasingly difficult to cope.

Late in 1956, Sara Jane made one of her very rare calls to her mother. She was clearly upset. She needed to have some time back home in West Virginia, she explained, and was going to bring the children for an extended visit. She booked a direct flight from Los Angeles to Columbus, Ohio, and as her brother Dana told me, he drove up from Charleston to collect Sara Jane and the kids at the airport.

The plane landed just before sunset, and Dana stood watching the ground crew roll a staircase up to the door just behind the gleaming wings. The door opened, and the first of a hundred passengers began to deplane. He said he watched them walk off, one after the other, into the waiting arms of friends and relatives. But where was Sara Jane? Finally, after all of the other passengers had left, little Sydney Jr., four years old, carefully walked down the steps, holding tight to the railing with one hand and grasping the hand of his three-year-old sister, Janet, in the other. Right behind him was a stewardess, holding nine-month-old baby Christopher in her arms. Dana watched, puzzled. Sara Jane was not with them.

The Kahns were shocked beyond belief. They were sure that something terrible had happened to Sara Jane. They called the airline, the hospitals, and the police. They called her home phone, but it had been disconnected. As the days went by with no call from Sara Jane, they even called Syd at his air base. He had no idea of his ex-wife's whereabouts, and he was not free to go searching. Finally, Ruth and Olaf realized that she was not hurt or sick. Sara Jane had carefully planned this maneuver, effectively abandoning her children to her mother's care.

Two and a half months passed before Sara Jane called home, collect, from a pay phone. Her parents begged her to come home and care for her three youngsters, pleading that her children needed their mother. Sara Jane promised to come home—she just needed a little more time. This scene was replayed several times over the next two months, with Sara Jane calling collect and promising to "come home soon." But she never did, and three months later, the calls stopped altogether.

After nearly a year, desperate, worn out, hurt beyond words, and hot with anger that their own child could behave in such a callous way, the Kahns tried to have Sara Jane arrested for failure to support her children. But even the police could not find her. Sara Jane had really disappeared this time.

Sydney Jr., Janet, and baby Christopher had landed on the Kahn's doorstep with a couple of shirts, some pants, one set of diapers, and a teddy bear. At age five, little Syd had some memory of leaving his mom in California and flying to West Virginia to live with his grandparents the year before. But for Janet and Chris, their grand-parents were their family. By now, only one of the Kahn children was living at home, fifteen-year-old Charlie. He would always be Uncle Charlie to the kids.

Ruth was forty-seven when the children arrived, and Olaf was fifty-seven and looking forward to retirement. They had college tuition for their own older children to think about, and raising three youngsters was a significant hardship. But Ruth and Olaf were the kind of people who did the right thing.

The Kahn home was still filled with books and music, but Ruth and Olaf raised their grandchildren just as they had raised their children: with little hugging and a lot of expectations. You had to obey all the rules or face the consequences. Ruth believed in a clean home and good manners. Olaf had high standards in terms of edu-cation, good behavior, and doing one's part. The dread of disap-proval weighed on the children as they struggled to please their grandparents.

"We lived in the world with permission and had to behave the way others expected us to behave," Chris told me. "We were taught to defer to everyone around us."

Ruth had become a strict Baptist and began attending Starcher Baptist Church on Twenty-sixth Street in Charleston. Starcher was part of the American Baptist Church, which has a history of opposing slavery and alcohol.

As Ruth became more involved with her church activities, Olaf continued on with DuPont, having reached a comfortable managerial position. He was at DuPont long enough to see proj-ects he had contributed to, such as his work on glycolic acid, make it all the way into the medical industry for use in helping to heal burn patients.

In the meantime, out of concern for the future of their grand-children, Olaf and Ruth had filed to legally adopt Sydney Jr., Janet, and Christopher. They published an announcement of the intended adoption in the vain hope that being faced with the formal loss of her children might flush out Sara Jane. Sara Jane's ex-husband, the children's father, had disappeared from their lives soon after the divorce and did not contest the adoption. The adoption also served the practical purpose of making the children eligible for Social Security survivors' benefits, to help meet the mounting expenses of raising three growing children if Olaf should die.

Olaf's career came to an unexpected halt when he suffered a nonfatal heart attack on the job in April 1964. As soon as he was well enough, Olaf applied for retirement, and within a month he was retired. Later that year, Olaf's heart finally gave out completely.

Skip told me his father was never one to sit around. The family had been growing corn in Saint Alban's, West Virginia, fifteen miles west of Charleston on the Kanawha River. "Dad was plowing the corn on a small Gravely tractor that had a vertical rotating plow," Skip told me in a conversation. "A neighbor to the farm said he saw Dad plowing. When he looked over later he heard the tractor running but it wasn't moving." The neighbor went to see what was going on.

"He said he found my Dad lying on the ground, not breathing. He called the police or the life squad, but Dad was dead."

Ruth, at fifty-eight, was left to raise a second family of three children, then aged thirteen, eleven, and eight.[4] Ruth clung to the church even more as an anchor by which to stabilize her life. She did not enforce discipline with anger; rather, she turned to the Bible and the fear of God as a way to control Syd, Janet, and Chris. She dominated her grandchildren in a way she could not dominate her own five children. Ruth, ever thinking ahead, moved with her grandchildren to Ohio to establish residency. The schools were better and she could be sure the kids would qualify to attend the state-funded Ohio state colleges.

The new family arrangement worked for a while with Janet and Chris. Syd, older when he arrived, maintained a certain amount of independence and managed to deflect Ruth's aim, but Janet became a devout Baptist while living at home, and Chris held on to the faith until high school. Chris, however, felt threatened by an angry God. "I was always afraid I was going to make Jesus mad," he told me. Ruth controlled the children by reminding them that Jesus was watching, so they had better behave.

Rather than cling to each other for support, Sara Jane's three children distanced themselves from each other, vying for approval within their new family. They each fought for parental favor for fear of losing their home again, and being cast out if they were not good enough.

Even so, Ruth and Olaf provided a refuge for their grandchildren and gave them a new family. But what they could never do was erase the rejection that the children would never understand.

When the kids were in their early twenties, their mythical mother blasted back into their lives from the radio, television, and newspapers as the woman who tried to kill the president.

The scars from those early years have never healed. One of the children told me, summing it up: "We are all broken."

THREE

THE DOCTOR'S WIFE

Sara Jane drove away from the airport after seeing her children off to their new lives in West Virginia and shrugged off her past like an old coat. When she disappeared from her family's lives, she created a new life for herself, and possibly even a new identity. Attempts to find documentation on the decade that followed this event were futile. Although she seems to have remained in Los Angeles from 1956 to 1966, only Sara Jane knows what she really did after she shipped her children off to live with her parents. She covered her tracks well as she hid from her family, and law enforcement could do little to help locate her. It is possible that she used aliases, and there is reason to believe that she used different Social Security numbers at various times.[1]

It is during the period from 1956 to 1963 that Sara Jane presumably went to school to study accounting, and worked to support herself. The details of this are unknown to me, but in trying to picture her in her late twenties, in the Los Angeles of the late 1950s, it is easy to envision a powerful young woman who was adept at making her own way in the world—charming, well-spoken, classy, and likely to impress a potential employer.

Sara Jane was familiar with the University of California at Los Angeles (UCLA) campus, as well as the streets of Westwood, and the location of the running track. Apparently, she took accounting classes at UCLA. I was unable to locate any records; but it is possible she registered under a different name. Sara Jane had her high school transcript sent to UCLA in 1950, and again in 1970. In a 1995 letter to me, she wrote: "When I was studying at UC there was a program that permitted one to start on graduate work while still an undergraduate." She went on to say in the letter that she had, in fact, begun work on her master's degree in just such a program while still an undergraduate. She loved to tell me stories about "running laps around the UCLA track and chatting" with Hollywood stars. The FBI reported that Sara Jane had almost completed a master's in business, but did not indicate at which school. The Office of the Registrar at UCLA found no records of Sara Jane Moore (or Kahn, or Manning, or Aalberg) ever completing a degree at UCLA.

With the onset of the sixties, Sara Jane found herself in a vastly changed world from the one in which she had abandoned her children. The cultural evolution from the conformist fifties to the authority-challenging new decade was dramatic. The bland Eisenhower era that she had lived in had crumbled. In 1963, civil rights worker Medgar Evers was murdered, and four little black girls died in a church bombing in Birmingham, Alabama. What was left of the fifties mind-set blew up completely in November of that year with the assassination of President John F. Kennedy in Dallas. But even before that, things were changing—and the signs were evident all over the country. Men no longer felt the need to wear fedoras. Women wore capri pants, and little girls wore pedal pushers. Small, foreign economy vehicles, such as Volkswagen Beetles and tiny Renault Dauphines, were slowly starting to replace some of the large, dependable American gas-guzzlers. In 1964, the Beatles led the British invasion in American music, displacing Elvis, the King, from his musical throne.

When the University of California at Berkeley added a new student union building to its campus in 1964, it not only changed the geography of the campus, but, in a series of almost accidental events, triggered the beginning of a movement that would capture the imagination of a generation.

Prior to the construction of the new building, Telegraph Avenue extended through the campus up to Sather Gate. Information tables with political position papers were stationed along Telegraph Avenue and often rallies were held there. Students handed out literature, sought signatures for petitions, and engaged in debate. With the construction of the Student Union building, however, Telegraph Avenue was truncated just east of the campus, at Bancroft Way. The traditional activities continued at this new gate to the campus.[2]

The adjacent sidewalks on Bancroft and Telegraph were generally regarded as city property. Groups received table permits from the city of Berkeley authorities. When there were questions about student activities on Telegraph Avenue, the Dean's Office referred them to the city police department. After the Student Union was built, the university changed its position and informed the heads of all student organizations that the Bancroft and Telegraph sidewalks were in fact university property and that all university rules would henceforth be applied. That meant no tables or speeches and only informational literature could be distributed; no advocacy was allowed. Immediately the students asked the school to reconsider and make the area available to the public rather than campus space.

Tension between the school administration and students grew. On December 2, 1964, the Associated Students of the University of California passed a "demonstration resolution." When their demands were not answered, students organized a sit-in and began pouring into Sproul Hall overnight. More than fifty on- and off-campus organizations banded together in joint protest of the Bancroft and Telegraph table ban.

Campus police showed up early on the morning of December 3 to try to restore order. In response, graduate student Mario Savio—who had just returned from civil rights actions in Selma, Alabama, and was still enraged by the injustices he had witnessed as a Freedom Rider—jumped on top of the police cruiser and gave an impromptu and impassioned speech:

> "There's a time," he said, "when the operation of the machine becomes so odious, makes you so sick at heart, that you can't take part; you can't even passively take part. And you've got to put your bodies upon the gears and upon the wheels, upon the levers, upon all the apparatus and you've got to indicate to the people who own it that unless you're free, the machines will be prevented from working at all."[3]

The students who had gathered in Berkeley that day began the Free Speech Movement, an explosion of political activism that tore through California and moved quickly across the country. In a show of support, Free Speech rallies occurred on university campuses less than a week later at Columbia University, City College, and Queens College in New York, as well as at Harvard University and the University of Michigan. The Movement set off a decade of challenges and rage that rattled the so-called establishment and gave rise to new role models for American youth. It put the concepts of equal rights, civil rights, and racial equality on everyone's lips and fostered a general contempt for anything standing in the way of peace and freedom.

Just as the country was going through a drastic transformation, this was also the case for Sara Jane. No longer a nurse, soldier, or housewife, in the early sixties Sara Jane drew on her accounting training and skills to reinvent herself as a bookkeeper at RKO studios in Hollywood. It was while working at RKO that she met John Aalberg, "Big John," as she called him, the man she later described as "the love of my life."

John O. Aalberg was born in Chicago in 1897,[4] the only son of Scandinavian immigrant parents. Sara Jane told everyone she met that he was a "heavyweight" in Hollywood; she called him "Big John" for many reasons. He was tall, a bit over six feet, with a welcoming face and a genuine smile that softened the hardest heart. A pair of tortoiseshell glasses were forever slipping down his nose, and instead of pushing them up with one finger, he would adjust the pesky frames from the side, giving him a refined air. When Sara Jane first met John, he had a full head of white hair, which was in stark contrast to his youthful face and buoyant style.

Professionally, Aalberg was a sound recordist and special effects expert—an early and well-known contributor to the refinement of sound in movies. Between 1936 and 1954, he was nominated for nine Academy Awards, including his sound recording for RKO's *Citizen Kane* (1941) and *It's a Wonderful Life* (1946). He received the Academy's Scientific/Technical Award in 1938, and would later win the Academy's Medal of Commendation for outstanding service in 1979. In 1982 he won the Gordon E. Sawyer Award for his lifetime contributions to the industry.[5] For Sara Jane, landing a man like "Big John" was a real coup.

Sara Jane thought of herself as the "new young girl" at RKO—despite the fact that she was already in her mid-thirties. Her success in playing that role, at least when it came to Aalberg, was helped by the fact that he was thirty-three years older than she and two years older than her own father.

Sara Jane first saw John from her desk when he visited the RKO administrative offices. Sara Jane soon found out that John was single and considered a man about town who was never without a date. Knowing that he was a bit of a womanizer only fueled Sara

Jane's determination to win him over. According to her version of the courtship, she decided to present herself as the prim and proper girl from West Virginia in contrast to the many would-be actresses looking for their big break that he was likely dating. She said that, at the time, she was living in a women-only hotel and that John had to get her back in time for an 11:00 P.M. curfew. She said she made it clear to him that she was not like other girls and maintained an air of propriety for a while.

"I decided that I wouldn't make it easy for him," she told me in a letter. "I made him work hard before I agreed to a first date with him, and then I didn't even let him kiss me goodnight that first time, which was totally unlike what he was used to with the other girls at the studios." She practiced being coquettish, explaining that she would first look down, and then glance up furtively. She called this her "proven technique."

"He was very used to getting what he wanted," she explained in another letter. "I played hard to get and that was how I reeled him in."

John landed with a thud. When he popped the question, Sara Jane said yes. They were married in June 1965. Sara Jane had three marriages and four children behind her; her parents were both alive, and she had four siblings. Yet, she wrote to me that on the night of his proposal, she looked up at Big John and said lovingly, "You know, one of the things we have in common is that neither of us has any family."[6]

Long after their breakup, Sara Jane would continue to brag about John to her friends. "He was a biggie in Los Angeles," she would say, nodding her head seriously. "You'd know him." She loved to describe in detail the expensive pearl and amethyst earrings he had had made especially for her; she also liked to recall how she and John loved to pack light for a quick trip, boasting that they could travel around the world with just one suitcase and one toiletry case each.

However, Sara Jane's movie romance had an unhappy and abrupt ending. In July 1965—just one month after their marriage, and shortly after she felt John's child quicken within her—Sara Jane packed her bags, dumped John, and headed up the coast to San Francisco. Alone. Afterward, she would say that she left "to think things over"; she detested Los Angeles and just could not stay there a minute longer. She never gave me a clear reason why she did not like Los Angeles, just that she could no longer live there. "We both assumed we would eventually end up back together," she wrote to me. "That we didn't is because of L.A."

Sara Jane's fifth child, Frederic W. Aalberg, was born in San Francisco on March 18, 1966.[7] For John, who really didn't have any other family, maintaining a link with his son was especially important. He and Sara Jane developed an informal custody and visitation agreement for Frederic that included child-care payments from John to Sara Jane in exchange for monthly weekend visits. John would visit Frederic every other month in San Francisco, and in the alternate months, Sara Jane would take the boy to Los Angeles to see his father. John even considered moving north, but his work was in Los Angeles and he could not leave. Sara Jane felt conflicted: Her beloved Big John was in Los Angeles, where she claimed to have had friends and good memories; yet she hated L.A. and felt "crushed and depressed" every time the plane landed at Los Angeles International Airport.

By the summer of 1967, the dam had broken as far as popular culture was concerned. Young people were streaming into Berkeley and San Francisco from all over the United States. An estimated 100,000 arrived, eager to join the hippies and become part of Haight-Ashbury's "Summer of Love." The psychedelic sixties were being celebrated everywhere from popular music to *Life* magazine.

Peace, love, and understanding were the words of the day. The generational conflict was raging, and there was nothing the older generation could do to influence kids who suddenly proclaimed that they didn't "trust anyone over thirty." In downtown San Francisco, the genteel ladies in white gloves who had sipped tea and shopped in Union Square for decades were unceremoniously replaced by their longhaired, face-painted daughters and sons who were experimenting with mind-expanding drugs and free love, caught up in the excitement and momentum of the times.

The north-south visits with Big John did not last long. Any thought Sara Jane might have had about reconciling did not last either. Frederic was only eighteen months old when, on December 22, 1967,[8] Sara Jane married Dr. Willard J. Carmel Jr., a man just ten years her senior. A mutual friend who made the introduction told Sara Jane that Carmel was a successful physician who worked for Kaiser Permanente, a major California health maintenance organization. A year earlier, Dr. Carmel had divorced his first wife, Helen, the mother of his two children.[9]

Feeling suddenly vulnerable and alone with a young child again, Sara Jane was looking to the safety of the suburbs. Carmel, a man with a strong presence and a forceful personality, made her feel secure. She knew that he would take care of her and her son. She honed in on her target and turned on her West Virginia charm. After the wedding, Carmel began to provide support for Sara Jane and Frederic, and he even insisted that Sara Jane discontinue receiving child support from Big John. Dr. Carmel did not want money coming from another man as a reminder of Sara Jane's past, Sara Jane told me in a letter.

Carmel moved Sara Jane and Frederic into a house in the new Sycamore development a few miles away from the center of

Danville. The pastoral, upper-middle-class community of perfectly maintained homes and strict codes, covenants, and restrictions helped maintain an orderly environment. It was a peaceful respite from the youth revolution that was beginning to shake the nation and the turmoil that was turning other parts of the San Francisco Bay Area inside out.

As Sara Jane began to remodel her new home, she met some of Willard's friends at the Blackhawk Country Club in Danville. Blackhawk was considered the most prestigious club in the East Bay. She was determined to fit in and talked endlessly to the wives about fixing her home, Sara Jane's Danville neighbors told me.

Sara Jane described the details of landscaping her home in Danville to me: She liked gardening and spent hours at the local nursery to find just the right shrubs and flowers to line the walkway to the front door. She told me the house was decorated in what she called Early Matron style, but she would transform it according to tasteful southern graciousness.

Slowly she began to meet the other women at the club. It appeared to Sara Jane that there were some rather significant contradictions between what these women said and what they did. While their conversations often focused on civil rights and current political issues, she told me that was as far as it went—just conversation.

As she began to take more of an interest in the outside world, she developed a low level of discomfort that she buried at the time. She could not explain clearly to me what exactly was bothering her. She simply told me that while she enjoyed fixing her home, she did not want to shut herself off from the rest of the world.

Sara Jane lived the paradox of discussing these topics while remaining an armchair observer. She could picture herself there on the front lines in the early 1960s in the fight to eliminate segregation. She could envision riding with the students on the buses in Washington, D.C., or at a lunch counter in Greensboro, sitting with other civil rights activists, defying the locals. As she learned more, she could see herself as an active participant. Sara Jane needed to change her strategy.

The civil rights movement had created a new consciousness in restaurants and clubs throughout the country. Waiters and waitresses in many restaurants were African American, and the white patrons and club members, uncomfortable with these obvious class differences, would reflect those feelings by being overly solicitous.

Groups of whites and blacks joined to show support for the civil rights activists in the South. New leaders began to emerge from several communities.

By the mid-sixties, frustration with the slow pace of civil rights change grew and began to merge with the general frustration about America's participation in the ongoing and seemingly endless Vietnam War. Nonviolent groups began to take a more militant stance. In 1966, joining alongside the mainly white Students for a Democratic Society (SDS) was the Black Panther Party (BPP), formed in Oakland, California—just a few miles from Danville—as part of the larger Black Power movement.

For the more conservative white citizens, Danville remained a refuge from the teeming demonstrators, brash bra-burning feminists, and long-haired hippies who were challenging the status quo on every street corner and government step. Danville and its neighboring Walnut Creek community were buffered from the harshness of San Francisco by distance, and from the political rudeness of Berkeley by the foothills. The Sycamore housing development was a testament to an upper-middle-class community that did not want the realities of the Vietnam War, women's rights, drugs, and antiestablishment challenges to enter their world. The heavily tree-lined streets and the pristine country club and tennis courts were all the reality they needed. In Danville, moms had their hair done, stayed home with their children, took tennis lessons, and kept well within the environs of their safe geography. It still seemed to be the early 1950s in Danville.

The members of an informal group of neighborhood moms nicknamed "the Danville Circle" were not very receptive to Sara Jane. "She was well kept and attractive. It wasn't that," complained one mother who at the time had five children under the age of ten. "It's that she barged in on my life as though I had nothing to do but listen to her. The final straw for me came one morning. Ms. Moore-Carmel showed up on my doorstep all charged up about one of her campaigns. She invited herself in without a thought to my schedule, settled into my kitchen, and just talked nonstop until I was late for a pediatrician appointment. I had to practically throw her out. She had no regard for anyone but herself."

Another member of the circle added: "She always wanted to be the center of everything . . . and always name dropping . . . that just made me so-o-o uncomfortable . . . no, actually, it's worse—she royally pissed me off!"

Sara Jane wanted to find a group of women who did meaningful work. She found projects for herself and sought to involve others in them. One such project was spearheading a collection for the family of a construction worker who had fallen and died while the subdivision was being completed. By 1970, even though she had been envisioning herself in the activist melee of the era, she had thrown herself headlong into the reelection campaign of Republican Senator George Murphy, an ultraconservative former song-and-dance man whose best-known accomplishment during his six years in Washington was having an always-full candy jar on his desk.

Sara Jane had been involved in the actor-candidate's first campaign during her Hollywood years. Murphy's election to the Senate in 1964 had been helped both by California's powerful supporters of conservative Barry Goldwater and by the weak campaign mounted by Democratic opponent Pierre Salinger; but Sara Jane felt that her support had helped significantly as well. When Sara Jane visited a number of her Danville neighbors to seek their support in Murphy's reelection campaign, she put herself front and center. "In true form," one neighbor reported, "Sara Jane elaborated her importance to the point that, to hear her tell it, Murphy had been elected in 1964 because of her."

In 1970, however, Sara Jane's determined support for Murphy was not quite enough to carry him to victory. His younger rival, John Tunney, a Kennedy look-alike, swept the election with a lopsided margin of victory of more than 600,000 votes. Sara Jane, too, was crushed and defeated.

FOUR

CHANGING TIMES

After the senatorial election of 1970, Sara Jane had no friends to turn to. Her aggressive campaigning had alienated most of the Danville circle, and they eventually cut her out of their play groups and babysitting pool; they also left the Carmels out of their adult social events. The mothers liked and felt empathy for six-year-old Frederic, though. "It's too bad about her little boy," one Danville neighbor said to me. "She dressed him up like an East Coast preppy doll, in short pants and knee-length socks. All the other kids made fun of him. We welcomed that very polite and well-mannered young man and made room for him when we could."

Sara Jane managed to find several teenaged girls who would babysit for Frederic when she and Willard went out in the evening, but she quickly became notorious among these teens as being very slow to pay. A number of the girls' mothers had to chase her down to collect for their daughters. Soon, these girls refused to sit for Frederic.

Sara Jane found a school in Walnut Creek for her son that she described as perfect for her needs: the Palmer School for Boys and Girls. Palmer was a private school, with tuition and fees upward of

$500 per month—quite a sum for that decade, reflective of the income of the community it served. Sara Jane especially liked the school, she told me, because it "offered 7:00 A.M. to 6:00 P.M. care—well, actually the school day there was 7:00 A.M. to 3:00 P.M. and they offered care from 3:00 P.M. to 6:00 P.M." Even better, to her mind, the school had a dormitory where students could board for up to two weeks at a stretch. If Sara Jane knew she would be out late, she would simply arrange for Frederic to spend the night at school.

Sara Jane continued to make enemies among her neighbors. One spring morning she blatantly went against community rules by painting her front door purple. She was unfazed by the fact that it violated the covenants of the Sycamore Homes Association, and she ignored the ire of her neighbors until repeated letters and notices eventually forced her to change the color of the door. When Sara Jane called the administrator's office to express her feelings on the matter, Jim Graham, one of the developers of the subdivision, and a founder of the association, told me what happened when he took the call. "I had to hold the phone away from my ear because she was screaming at me at the top of her voice," Graham related. "And I was embarrassed that the women in the office had to hear that intense anger, expressed in such extremely foul language."

By 1970, on the macro level, the entire country was smoldering as the United States was losing a war of questionable value and validity in Vietnam. The war had turned brother against brother. In Berkeley, students and nonstudents were demonstrating against the war, and tear gas was flowing freely.

On the social front, women who sought liberation from centuries of oppression shocked their communities by demanding equal pay for equal work.

For many—women and men alike—social norms were, depending upon one's perspective, either eroding or evolving. The

world had become an arena of opportunity for anyone and everyone. Nothing was off-limits in terms of language, behavior, or
possibility.

With its refusal to withdraw from the war under public pressure, the Nixon Administration became a visible and fair target,
and many U.S. citizens were taking it on. College campuses became
the focus for outspoken activists challenging the status quo.

The anticapitalist, antiwar movement known as the New Left
set radical standards of taste and behavior. It was galvanized by an
unpopular war, the surge of a nationwide student uprising, and opposition to building more bombs. The Radical Education Project,[1]
formed in 1966 by the Students for a Democratic Society, sought to
create long-distance antiwar and radical political study groups.

In order to facilitate the recruitment of new members, SDS
member Paul Buhle and his wife, historian Mari Jo Buhle, started a
publication called *Radical America*, a newsletter of "American Radical History and Political Thought." The Buhles moved to the University of Wisconsin in the fall of 1967 and recruited several
members of the local SDS chapter to work on the journal.

By 1968 there had been a significant shift in the student
movement as well as populations in and around university towns.
College students led the way as an increase in activism led to a
mass student movement.[2] They filled basements with study
groups and plotted ways to get heard—or at least noticed—by
any means at all.[3]

Each new generation finds a way to carve out a place for itself,
driven by internal pressure to reinvent society. What set the seventies generation apart from their parents—the great majority of
whom chose without question to serve God and country during
the more law-abiding thirties, forties, and fifties—was primarily
the collision of an unpopular war with sweeping youth rebellion
against anything that seemed remotely status quo, fed by a new
sense of individual and group power.

By the early 1970s, the mood of peace and love that had characterized the 1960s was long gone. Both Bobby Kennedy and Martin Luther King Jr. had been assassinated, and with their passing went much of the idealism of their young followers. Many of the gentle, long-haired hippies who had flooded the streets of San Francisco in 1967 had fallen prey to drugs that were much more dangerous than LSD and marijuana. Methamphetamines and heroin turned many of them into street people. This lost generation was joined by runaways and Vietnam veterans who returned from the brutal and seemingly endless war in Southeast Asia demoralized, bitter, and often addicted to drugs and traumatized. Members of a generation that had been asked—or drafted—to fight a counterrevolutionary war now expressed their displeasure loud and clear: They said no to the war. Many said no to their parents, husbands, wives, children, friends, and country as well. This reaction caused a seismic shift that, perhaps inadvertently, led to years of violence in the United States.

The New Left embraced a collection of issues that claimed to support democratic principles and end such injustices as poverty, racial discrimination, and class distinctions.

People who identified themselves with the New Left were not all members of a single organization and there was disagreement among them on the mission as well as the methods of the movement. Its members ranged from pacifists to violent revolutionaries. There were those who practiced nonviolent civil disobedience. At times, these nonviolent believers were among the first to lead actions that became bloody clashes with the police.

The names and missions of the various revolutionary organizations claiming to be righting the wrongs of the government proliferated. It was becoming difficult for outsiders to determine the differences among them, or where they fit in the larger picture. Some picketed peacefully while others bombed government buildings and raced to claim responsibility.

Several political organizations grew out of the SDS. In 1969, the most militant wing of the SDS was the fledgling Weatherman group—who had named themselves after the lyrics of Bob Dylan's "Subterranean Homesick Blues": "You don't need a weatherman to know which way the wind blows." They issued a manifesto eschewing nonviolence and calling instead for armed opposition to U.S. policies. The Weathermen advocated the overthrow of capitalism, urging white radicals to trigger a worldwide revolution by fighting in the streets. Bombing government buildings was one of the ways they sought recognition. Another spin-off of the SDS, the New World Liberation Front, was composed of mostly white, middle-class students and some African American ex-cons. The group took credit for twenty-three bombings in northern California.

The SDS continued to splinter into multiple groups, all of whom wanted to bring the U.S. government into compliance with their various demands, whether it was for an end to the Vietnam War or for the eradication of racial oppression. The Radical Youth Movement focused on outreach to younger people, the Southern Student Organizing Committee was created to empower southern African Americans, and the Worker-Student Alliance advocated student involvement in workers' struggles both on and off campus. Several groups blamed the Weathermen for causing the split within the SDS. They were widely accused of terrorism and of giving all activists, both militant and mainstream, a bad name.[4]

The Weathermen spoke of "necessary violence," which attracted members who were tired of going through the traditional, peaceful channels to accomplish their goals. Former SDS leader Bernadine Dohrn led the Radical Youth Movement, and publicly announced a "declaration of war." When a bomb accidentally detonated in a Manhattan townhouse in 1970, the Weathermen went underground, disappearing into America and changing their name to the Weather Underground Organization. The evolution and proliferation of copycat bombing by revolutionaries soon made one group virtually indistinguishable from another.

Why was there so much violence? Why did so many organizations suddenly seek new ways to express their anger at law enforcement, corporate control, and illegal wars? Some historians point to the murders of Black Panthers Fred Hampton and Mark Clark in December 1969. The killings occurred during a Chicago police raid, and many people were sure that they were government-sanctioned actions meant to cripple the Black Panthers.[5]

Politics was not the only thing that was changing. Hard-edged punk and disco music replaced the folk songs that pleaded for peace and understanding, providing a sound track for an America that had grown into a different and sometimes frightening place to live.

Sara Jane watched the nightly news with growing concern. Every night there were more visions of death and futility. Danville, however, was still quiet and Republican. It was no longer a place that Sara Jane Kahn Anderson Moore Aalberg Carmel wanted to be.

From the start, Sara Jane wrote me, she could not "be one of those people that move to the suburbs and quits reading the newspapers just because the news is disturbing to me." In addition, the news she was reading about was of social revolution—women's rights, workers' rights, prisoners' rights, and the groups who were looking to bring about a major restructuring of the American government along more socialist lines.

Sara Jane started her own personal revolution when she filed for divorce from Willard Carmel in September 1971. This filing was the first step on a long and torturous path leading to the end of their marriage. Willard had a take-charge personality that made him an excellent physician, according to a Danville resident. Sara Jane felt taken care of at first, as she connected with Willard, infant Frederic in hand, but she eventually found his protectiveness suffocating. Willard was enchanted by Sara Jane's wit and her candor, but these same traits later led to constant confrontations between them. After the separation, and during a long and rancorous battle over the terms of a divorce, Sara Jane and Frederic continued to live in Willard's house, while Willard moved into a nearby condominium.

Sara Jane's suburban Republican years were over. Although she was too old to be a baby boomer, and she had previously supported conservative Republican causes, her head and her heart were now in perfect alignment with the radical youth politics of the time.[6] While Sara Jane had waged a rearguard battle with Willard Carmel over the spoils of their breakup, she was not just sitting idle in the house. She was becoming more politically active on several fronts.

She often left the confines of Danville to drive to events in Berkeley, including performances by Native American comedians at the Julia Morgan Theater and lectures on class struggle at the Glide Memorial Church in San Francisco. Although she never participated in the drug culture—it was always important to her to remain clear-headed—she enjoyed the excitement and stimulation of the new political movements and the feeling that she was participating in something important.

Her son Frederic was generally an afterthought when she made plans to be out. One night, when she got a last-minute minute call to attend an activity in the city, she became frustrated and upset because no one would sit for Frederic. Undeterred, she marched into the Danville Episcopalian Church with Frederic in hand. Sara Jane introduced herself to the Reverend George Ridgeway by announcing that she was an Episcopalian, and that the church had never done anything for her.

"It is time for the church to do something for us now," she said, her blue eyes piercing him with righteous indignation, "and that's to watch my son overnight because I have an important meeting to attend." Stunned, but not intimidated, Reverend Ridgeway graciously said that he would be pleased to have Frederic as a guest. He settled young Frederic into the spare room behind the sanctuary, and helped him unpack the overnight bag Sara Jane had prepared. Ridgeway then found some canned hot dogs and beans for dinner, read to him from the Bible, and put the child to bed. When he was telling me about this incident, Ridgeway described the boy as "a delightful young man," but one who had spoken very little.

Rather than being gone overnight, as she had expected, Sara Jane returned to Danville at about 11:00 P.M. She insisted on waking Frederic from a sound sleep at the church to take him home. Ridgeway never saw them again. Apparently, the church had now done something for Sara Jane.

As Sara Jane was no longer accountable to Willard, she spent more and more time driving back and forth to the larger Bay Area community. The new generation of people shouting, marching, and taking to the streets, which Sara Jane had been watching on the news as she had been decorating her home, looked a lot more interesting than life in Danville.

Sara Jane's dissatisfaction with the government had grown significantly in response to the layers of transparent lies that unraveled in the early 1970s. Sara Jane tended to live in rigid categories of black and white, and so the Watergate scandal turned her strong distrust of Washington into an even more powerful antipathy.

She began trying on new identities to go along with her emerging new life. She began to morph from the Republican, George Murphy–supporting doctor's wife into something very different. As she began to dip her toe into the cultural revolution that had been developing around her, her views of mainstream politics continued to sour. Like so many other women in those years of consciousness-raising groups and personal liberation, she began for the first time to start to pay more attention to politics and issues outside of her own personal world. She even worked as a volunteer at a free clinic in a medically underserved black section of Oakland.

In 1973, for the first time, Sara Jane went to march in support of César Chávez and the United Farm Workers. There she met Father Bill O'Donnell, a well-known activist priest. It would be a long association.

William O'Donnell was a Bay Area native, one of seven children in a family that sharecropped a farm in the Altamont Hills just east of Livermore. At his ordination into the priesthood in 1956, Father Bill was a conservative Eisenhower Republican. By 1965, however, he had visited Mississippi and Alabama, where he had seen the overt injustices of racism in the South; with his eyes more fully opened, he started to notice more subtle forms of racism in California. He also became deeply committed to the nonviolent approaches of Gandhi and Martin Luther King Jr. as a means for making changes in society.

O'Donnell learned about César Chávez and his work with the United Farm Workers (UFW) in 1966, when Chávez supported the fruit workers in Starr County, Texas, and led a march to Austin as a show of support. Chávez had formed the UFW to address the plight of migrant workers. The two men finally met at a state senate committee hearing. Afterward, O'Donnell said, he "was in awe of this little guy," and of Chávez associates Fred Ross and Dolores Huerta.

Chávez realized that trying to achieve success by traditional union means, coordinating multiple labor strikes at widely dispersed farms, would be very difficult. As an alternative, he developed and implemented the brilliant strategy of bringing consumer and retailer pressure to bear on the growers by organizing a highly effective national boycott of California table grapes. As people all over the United States stopped buying grapes, the farm owners began to feel squeezed.

O'Donnell began to support Chávez, and it was this support that drew the formerly conservative priest into his first act of civil disobedience. O'Donnell handed out leaflets and picketed. On May 15, 1969, in response to a direct and personal request from Chávez to join that day's protest, O'Donnell mentally prepared himself to be arrested.

O'Donnell joined the UFW team that met with Safeway Supermarket executives that afternoon at the company's Oakland headquarters. The UFW demanded that the grocery chain honor the grape boycott. Safeway executives refused; then they declared the meeting adjourned and walked out of the room. O'Donnell and a half dozen union members stayed in the room for four more hours, after which the company called the police. This was the priest's first arrest. His continuing nonviolent activist support for civil and humanitarian rights, his commitment to "standing up for causes when others looked the other way," would lead to some 224 additional arrests for him over the next thirty-three years.

Although O'Donnell was a rough-and-tumble Irish priest, who once told a reporter he was "kicked out" of three parishes before finding his rightful home, he was also popular among women because of his stand on equal rights. He found a home at a Berkeley church as assistant pastor. Under Father Bill's guidance, St. Joseph the Worker Church became a gathering place for activists working for social justice.

As the Carmels' divorce proceedings got underway, financial problems were exposed that went well beyond slow babysitter payments. As the accountant in the family, Sara Jane had taken over handling the responsibility for paying bills such as the mortgage, homeowner's dues, and yearly income taxes. Sara Jane had neglected the latter. Public records show that there were two government liens on the house due to unpaid federal income taxes for 1970 and 1972. Willard could not sell the house until the liens were satisfied.

Sara Jane had also never paid the Sycamore Homes Association dues. From her perspective, if the association would not let her paint her door any color she wanted, they were going to have to "whistle Dixie" to get dues from her.

Sara Jane's divorce was complicated and messy. In California, community property accrued during the marriage is generally simply split in half. This tends to make divorce settlements relatively straightforward, and the complete documentation for many California divorces runs to just a dozen pages or so. Not so for Sara Jane. The Contra Costa Superior Court record on the Carmel's divorce action is 201 pages long, and that does not even count the multiplicity of court-destroyed background memos.

Sara Jane was the petitioner for the divorce, and Willard Joseph Carmel, Jr. the respondent. The papers stated that the marriage had lasted three years and eight months, and there were no children from the marriage. Sara Jane filed for spousal support of $950 a month, for property rights (e.g., sole occupancy of the home), and for attorney fees of $500.

In her listing of family property, she included the Walnut Creek Convalescent Home. Willard had been one of several owners of that facility since long before his marriage to Sara Jane, but she envisioned herself as part owner and believed that she could get some good money from her perceived community property interest in the facility. A "show cause" date of October 8, 1971, was set for Willard's response to the petition. The filing also requested temporary orders restraining Willard from transferring any property and from entering the home.

On October 15, 1971, the court issued a temporary order under which Sara Jane was allowed to stay in the home during the divorce process, but was responsible for the mortgage payments on it. She received $400 each month in temporary spousal support and $700 for legal fees.

The court also issued a temporary restraining order that enjoined Willard and Sara Jane from harassing one another. Included in the paperwork that Sara Jane filed in support of her request for a restraining order were statements that she feared that Willard might try to sell the property and claiming that in the past he had used physical force—striking and threatening her.

On February 27, 1972, the court issued a summons to Sara Jane to appear for a deposition on March 29. The summons directed her to bring documents that were essential and relevant to the case, including checking account statements and other financial records. Sara Jane did not produce the financial records for that deposition.

On May 2, 1972, Carmel's attorney, Terrance Ring, dropped a bombshell: He filed a "nullity allegation" stating that there was reason to believe that the marriage should be annulled rather than terminated by divorce.

Richard Johnson, who had taken over as Sara Jane's attorney on April 27, petitioned the court on May 5 for a delay in the scheduled trial. He indicated that he had been informed, when he took on the case, that it was "substantially ready" for trial, but he had discovered that (1) it was not ready for trial; (2) the records necessary for the trial to move forward had not been located; (3) respondent Willard claimed separate property interests from those suggested by Sara Jane's filing; and (4) the respondent was seeking relief under the nullity provisions of the law. Attorney Ring did not object to the request for a delay; it was agreed that any support order would be retroactive to June 1.

On July 24, 1972, the court issued its decision: Based on the evidence, the marriage was annulled. The court based its decree of nullity on the grounds of a preexisting marriage, with the following explanation: "That at the time of the marriage petitioner was still legally married to a John Aalberg; that said marriage was valid and subsisting at the time of the petitioner's marriage to respondent, the same not having been dissolved." That is, Sara Jane had not gotten divorced from John before she married Willard.

The court told Sara Jane that she could live in the house for up to six months, during which time the house was to be sold and the proceeds divided. There had been a delay between the July hearing and the formal entering of the judgment. A final judgment of nullity was entered on February 15, 1973.

The court order included the judgment of nullity; the restoration of Sara Jane Carmel's name to Sara Jane Aalberg; an order for the house to be sold within six months; monthly payments of $400 as spousal support for a maximum of six months (to cease sooner if the house was sold sooner); and the statement that the interest in the convalescent home fully belonged to Willard.

Sara Jane would not move out of the house, and she stopped making payments on the mortgage. She dug in for the long haul. She filed an appeal of the judgment of nullity on April 23, 1973. Her attorney queried the court about the cost of receiving a written transcript of the court proceedings. On May 20, she received a letter indicating the price would be $248. Through yet another attorney, Sara Jane complained about the cost of that transcript and filed to have Willard pay for the transcript so she could prosecute her appeal. On July 6, 1973, the request to have Willard pay for the transcript was denied. However, the court issued a stay on the orders to sell the house pending the appeal.

In November 1973, seven months after she was informed of the price of receiving the transcript, and four months after having been told that Willard did not have to pay for it, Sara Jane sent a check to the courts for $248. She received a letter back indicating that, as she had not responded within ten days, the appeal had been formally dismissed. Sara Jane was told to put the house up for sale forthwith.

By January 1974, Sara Jane had still taken no action to sell the house. Frustrated, Willard went back to court, seeking to get Sara Jane evicted or, at the least, to force her to get a move on.

In response to Carmel's request, the court appointed Donald G. Sherwood as referee and charged him with managing the sale of the house. The court also indicated that, if either party was not willing to sign the necessary listing agreement for the house, the court would direct such a signature and, if the order was not obeyed, the court would exercise its authority to sign for the party or parties involved.

Sherwood selected the Ray Taylor Real Estate Company to implement the sale. Ray Taylor went to see the house in order to prepare materials for the sale, but Sara Jane refused to let him in.

Sherwood called Sara Jane to find out why she refused Taylor entry. She responded, saying, "I have an attorney (now Richard K. Critchlow), and I have been instructed to refer all calls dealing with the court to my attorney."

A week later, Sara Jane sent a long letter to the court indicating that, as far as she was concerned, she had moved forward to sell the house. She had talked to people in the community in order to get recommendations on a real estate agent, and she had now signed a listing agreement with an agent. Sherwood determined that she had sought to get the agent to accept the listing and file it with the Multiple Listing Service with only her own signature— that is, without Willard's required signature as well, and without regard to the court-referee-appointed real estate agent. Sara Jane needed Sherwood's approval if she was to get her own real estate agent, and she needed to advise the court if she were to do so; she did neither.

The house went into foreclosure in May 1974. However, the foreclosure was forestalled and the house finally sold. Sara Jane and Willard split the net proceeds of $17,000.

Now, with no income and no home, Sara Jane was forced to leave Danville.

FIVE

SAN FRANCISCO'S RADICAL UNDERGROUND

The halls of Vacaville prison extend in opposite directions; so far out that it seems infinite. Inmates are housed in cells within the immense complex and form communities with their brothers to better cope with the vastness of the institution. The Symbionese Liberation Army (SLA) formed as the result of outside visitation programs that supported the Black Cultural Association (BCA), founded in 1968. Its purpose was to offer "alternatives to the Black Offender in his apathy and to deal with the unique problems that confront him inside the prisons."[1]

BCA had thirty volunteer tutors, mostly from the University of California at Berkeley, who went to the prison to conduct educational programs in math, reading and writing, art, history, political science, black sociology, and African heritage. Within the prison the group began to grow, eventually meeting three times a week. The tutorial program also gained popularity in Berkeley, attracting additional volunteers from the university, as well as the attention of interested observers in the community at large. In 1971, Vacaville prison hired Colston Westbrook to coordinate the BCA program. Westbrook was a linguistics instructor at UC Berkeley. He spoke Italian, French, German, Korean, and Japanese.

Westbrook became involved in the issue of prisoners' rights. He was in demand for consulting about the well-regarded BCA program, as well as for his extensive language skills. Before going to Vacaville, Westbrook had served in the army for three years and in the air force for four. Although he tried to keep his military background private, many in the BCA passed along exotic tales about Westbrook's military service, saying that he was more than just a serviceman, that he had done and continued to do work for the Central Intelligence Agency that involved brainwashing, and that he was using and teaching brainwashing techniques at Vacaville.

Donald DeFreeze was serving a five-year sentence for armed robbery and was a BCA member. After three and a half years at Vacaville, he was transferred to Soledad prison, from which he escaped in June 1973. After his escape, he formed the Symbionese Liberation Army to force changes in the prison system. He used the stories that Westbrook was a CIA operative to help recruit people to work with him against the existing prison system. DeFreeze adopted the title General Field Marshall Cinque Mtume; he was commonly referred to as Cinque (pronounced "san-cue").[2]

The SLA conspired to kidnap the heiress Patty Hearst as a means to raise money. The plot was hatched by Cinque with fellow revolutionary Theo Wheeler. Wheeler was a major player in another organization, Venceremos,[3] named after an idealistic American youth group that had traveled to Cuba during the 1960s to cut sugarcane. Other targets identified for potential kidnappings included members of other prominent families, such as the Vanderbilts, Du Ponts, and Rockefellers.[4] Patty Hearst, living away from her family in her apartment in Berkeley, was an easy target, and her father had and could provide the money they needed to feed and supply the army.[5]

Cinque gathered a cadre of volunteers for the operation from among the people who had been teachers and helpers for the BCA. Among those whom Cinque molded into the initial group of SLA soldiers were Patricia Soltysik and Emily Harris. Soltysik, who was studying at UC Berkeley on a state scholarship, had become embittered by what she saw as an oppressive socioeconomic system. She was a radical feminist and had put her plans for law school on hold until the time when all women were free. In 1971, she attached herself to the radical group of ex-convicts called the United Prisoners Union and dropped out of school completely. Soltysik's lover, Camilla Hall, gave her the nickname "Mizmoon."

Emily Harris, the daughter of an engineer, had graduated from Indiana University with a bachelor's degree in language arts; she was a straight "A" student and member of the honor society. While at Indiana, she had received training from the CIA. She and her husband, Bill Harris, worked for the Indiana State Police Department, setting up narcotics arrests, until they moved to the San Francisco Bay Area in the spring of 1973.

Other SLA members included Wendy Yoshimura, a Japanese American woman born in Manzanar, an American internment camp in California during World War II. Wendy was a Berkeley radical who was running from a 1972 bombing charge. Berkeley locals William Wolfe, Robyn Steiner, and Russell Little became part of the SLA as well.

William "Willy" Wolfe grew up on the East Coast, the son of an anesthesiologist. He attended prep schools and was a National Merit Scholarship finalist. Wolfe moved to Berkeley in 1971 to attend school. He enrolled in a program on Afro-American Studies sponsored by UC Berkeley and decided to do his term paper on the BCA project at Vacaville. It was through the associations he made at Vacaville and the BCA that Wolfe joined with the terrorist group. He was charged with raping Patty Hearst after the group kidnapped her. She (as Tania) eventually became his lover.[6] He died with five other SLA members, including Hall and Soltysik, in a televised shootout with police on May 17, 1974.

The SLA's aim eventually broadened beyond prison reform to a desire to revolutionize the American political system. The chosen methods were direct and criminal: assassinations, kidnappings, and bank robberies. Cinque constructed a violent strategy for what he called a "new Marxist revolution." The SLA's first public act was the murder of Marcus Foster, the black Oakland superintendent of schools. Foster was a progressive with a national reputation for educational excellence, and he was respected by diverse constituencies for his good work in the Oakland schools. His killing, given his reputation, was puzzling to many. Apparently, the SLA "mistakenly believed Foster wanted to require students to show identification on campus, which it believed analogous to a police-state tactic."[7]

According to author Vin McLellan in *The Voices of Guns*, the SLA's goals had "nothing to do with changing the political aspects of society. It was all about personal goals. The SLA was nothing more than hubris. They took an emotional experience and turned it into a psycho-political experience that had nothing to do with reality. They accomplished nothing more than getting themselves and others killed."[8]

The goal of the strong and multiethnic prisoners' rights movement that evolved in the 1970s was to improve the treatment of prisoners and ensure that they could earn decent wages. At the time, California inmates who were allowed to work were earning very little—between two and sixteen cents an hour. Programs were also developed and staffed by volunteers to educate prisoners, both while behind bars and when released, to try to prevent recidivism. While the prison reform movement was full of ex-cons who created dual identities as revolutionaries and crusaders for the prison reform cause, there was much general sympathy and support for the movement both inside and outside prison walls. Many San Francisco political groups joined the prisoners' rights band-wagon—including the SLA and the little-known but very impor-tant Tribal Thumb group, a twenty-five-member bank robbery and revolutionary group led by ex-con Earl Satcher. Satcher had served eighteen years in prison for armed robbery, assault, and illegal gun possession.[9]

The prison labor movement originated at Soledad Prison, and then spread to Folsom State Prison, where prisoners held a seven-teen-day strike in November 1970, seeking the legal minimum wage and workmen's compensation benefits for inmate workers. The movement got play for a good part of the decade. However, in 1977 it was effectively shut down by a Supreme Court decision that refused to extend First Amendment constitutional protection to prison unions.

The idea of the prisoner as revolutionary caught the public imagination and was fueled by the writings of Soledad prison in-mate George Jackson, founder of the inmate revolutionary group known as the Black Guerrilla Family. Jackson became known for his inspiration in spite of his incarceration. Jackson had been con-victed of robbing a gas station of seventy dollars in his early teens and was given an indeterminate sentence of one year to life. His books, *Soledad Brother* and *Blood in My Eye*, offer riveting tales of black oppression and are highly regarded by historians.[10] Prison guards at San Quentin killed Jackson on August 21, 1971, in what the state claimed was an escape attempt. Many witnesses said Jack-son was not trying to escape and that the guards were looking for an opportunity to "get" him.

Jackson's writings were required reading among the politically radical in the 1970s San Francisco Bay Area. The romance of Jack-son's inspired philosophy coming from inside prison held particu-larly powerful influence with students of Mao. The concept of nonviolent protest, according to Jackson, did not work. "It may serve our purpose to claim nonviolence, but we must never delude ourselves into thinking that we can seize power from a position of weakness, with half measures, polite programs, righteous indignation, and loud entreaties."[11]

During this time, a number of prisoners—many of them black—felt drawn to the Black Power movement that had supplanted the more peaceful civil rights movement. Suddenly, there were radicals inside the prisons who called themselves "revolutionaries." They were, moreover, revolutionaries who embraced violence.

On the outside, in the Bay Area between 1972 and 1974, political violence took on a sinister and personal tone. A series of seventy-one vicious unsolved murders occurred in San Francisco. Police code-named them "Zebra" because the dedicated radio channel used by the police investigating the case was channel Z— "Zebra" in radio talk. Reporters soon got wind of the moniker and started writing about the "Zebra murders."

The Zebra killers attended the Nation of Islam temple at Fillmore and Geary Streets in San Francisco. This small cadre called themselves the Death Angels and they systematically stalked and killed whites to earn points in heaven.[12]

The group was formed in October 1973 when a small group of disaffected ex-con black males became angry at how white society consistently singled them out no matter what happened on the street. They joined an organization called Black Self-Help, a group that helped members to find jobs and places to live. The group's activities quickly evolved into planning of the Zebra killings. Key members were present to hatch their diabolical plans, each feeding off the others' ideas of how best to punish the "blue-eyed white devils." One plan developed by the Zebra group was to blow up school buses by placing dynamite in their exhaust pipes. On the way to school, when the buses were filled with children and the dynamite had a chance to sweat, the buses would explode and likely affect cars near the buses as well as the children who were riding in them. However, that idea was abandoned because of the possibility that black kids might be on the buses or in the cars.

Another idea was to get a high-powered rifle, drive to a road near an airport, and try to shoot down an airplane as it was taking off. That idea was also scrapped as there might be Muslims in the aircraft. Finally, it was decided that the only way to eliminate the white devil was by direct attack. That way there would be no mistake or error resulting in the killing of blacks or Muslims. The first victims in this wave of violence were Richard and Quita Hague. The Hagues, an elderly couple out for a walk, were abducted at gunpoint, forced into a van, and bound. Richard was beaten over the head with a lug wrench, but somehow survived. He told the police that his wife, Quita, was raped and hacked with a machete as she begged for her life. Quita was nearly decapitated.[13]

The violent and cowardly gunpoint attacks continued, and more people died. The victims were mostly women and weak or elderly men who could not fight back. The case took on a more sinister meaning as it became apparent that the killings were not random and unconnected. White people in San Francisco were terrified. As news spread of the increasingly grisly attacks, older couples—the main targets—began to ask for police escorts whenever they left their offices or homes. Talk of black-on-white hate crime abounded, and violent arguments ensued in the streets.

In the end, several of the Zebra killers were caught in San Francisco when one of those involved ratted out the others to save his own skin. Other Death Angels who had operated in other cities were never caught.[14]

The killings created a division between the Nation of Islam and the revolutionary Black Panthers. Many members of the latter group did not agree with the tactics of the Death Angels. While the Black Panthers were at war with white law enforcement, they

were not at war with civilian white Americans and did not participate in random kidnapping and torture.[15]

The Black Panthers' Ten Point Mission to create community
programs and encourage education was disrupted by a violent
shootout with police. Although the group was short-lived, the Panthers had a major impact on the black community and society in
general.

The generation of young adults living in America in the 1970s had
been radicalized and desensitized by assassinations, urban riots,
and antiwar demonstrations.[16] One of the results was the formation of political organizations that targeted the status quo of the
American class structure. The mission of these groups was to end
the oppression of the working class and to stop war. Their tactics
for implementing change ranged from educating people and gaining public office to acts of violence. More than seventy bombings
shook the foundations of government and corporate office buildings in the Bay Area.

The country was hurtling through a transformation of social
values. Frederick Dutton, a historian and cabinet member under
President John F. Kennedy, wrote in his 1972 book, *Changing Sources
of Power,* "The key political struggle of the decade could well turn
out to be as much over the nature of our culture as the politics of the
1930s were over the nature of the economy. The underlying campaigns likely to go on are indicated by the contending slogans
'Make the World Safe for Sex' and 'Support Your Local Censor.'"[17]

Major strides had also been made in the fight for racial equality during the preceding decade, beginning with the Civil Rights
Act of 1964, the Voting Rights Act of 1965, and such legal decisions as *Loving v. Virginia,* 388 U.S. 1 (1967), in which antimisce-
genation laws were declared unconstitutional.

Many veterans of the Black Power movements of the 1960s—some of whom were still in jail—continued the battle in a variety of ways. Their approaches ranged from economic and social integration and mainstream public leadership roles to radical and often violent activities.[18]

Some African Americans who had been on the front lines, in both the antiwar movement and in the battle for civil rights, simply blended into the general working- and middle-class populace, holding jobs, buying homes, and raising families. They sought equality through a basic capitalist model of earning one's way into the mainstream. Others used the new laws as a springboard to the public and political stage.

Willie Brown was elected to the California State Assembly in 1965. The first black Assembly member from San Francisco, Brown would serve as a powerful speaker of the chamber for fifteen years, and then as mayor of San Francisco. The Reverend Cecil Williams became the minister of San Francisco's Glide Memorial Church in 1963. The Glide Church was and still is a widely respected champion of those with very limited means.

On the national level, Andrew Young, who had worked as an assistant to Martin Luther King Jr. during the civil rights movement, was elected in the early seventies as the first black southern congressman since Reconstruction. Young served three terms in the House before being appointed ambassador to the United Nations. He was then elected mayor of Atlanta, and his public service continues as this book is written.

While many African Americans merged into mainstream economic, social, and political arenas, certain activist groups became more radical. Three types of people flowed into these fringe groups. One was comprised of African Americans who had been in prison. A second was made up of disaffected African Americans who came back from Vietnam feeling that they had been disproportionately used to fight in a racist war, and for a country that was still racist. The third was an influx of young people in their twenties, liberal, college-educated, primarily female, middle- to upper-class whites. Most joined because they had a strong sense of social justice; for others, the draw was the opportunity to actively challenge the forbidden interclass and interracial conventions of the time.

There was a dynamism, an intensity of energy in the radical organizations that was attractive to many middle-class liberals who sought to become part of the adventure, of this revolution fought by ex-convicts and others willing to live on the edge. Three radical groups that evolved were the United Prisoners Union, the Symbionese Liberation Army, and Tribal Thumb. All three groups were strongly influenced by the prisoners' rights movement and the writings of George Jackson; all three came to play a significant role in Sara Jane's life.

SIX

THE WOULD-BE ACTIVIST

On February 4, 1974, Sara Jane Moore read an article in her morning paper that would change her life. It reported that a radical terrorist group calling itself the Symbionese Liberation Army (SLA) had kidnapped nineteen-year-old college student Patricia Hearst, the daughter of publisher Randolph Hearst and granddaughter of newspaper magnate William Randolph Hearst, from her Berkeley apartment. Like most people who read the news that day, Sara Jane had never heard of the SLA. She did not know, and the paper did not say, what *Symbionese* meant, who the group's members were, where they were from, or what they really wanted.

The first question was easily and quickly answered. Donald De-Freeze, a member of the Black Cultural Association (BCA), was sentenced to a five-year term at Vacaville prison for armed robbery. He was frustrated with the prison system, which kept promising reforms that never came. DeFreeze was transferred to Soledad prison, from which he escaped in June 1973. He then began forming what he called an "army," the SLA, to force changes in the prison system. Defreeze wrote in his manifesto that the the name *symbionese* is taken from the word *symbiosis,* and he defined its meaning as "a body

of dissimilar bodies and organisms living in deep and loving har-
mony and partnership in the best interest of all within the body."[1]
The SLA symbol was a seven-headed cobra. Each head represented
a principle of Kwanzaa.[2]

The rest of story was not so easy to understand. The kidnapping of Patty Hearst struck Sara Jane, as it did others when the
news broke, as bizarre. As details emerged, the story only got
stranger. As police fanned out all over the Bay Area in search of the
kidnapped heiress, Sara Jane devoured every word of the daily
newspaper coverage, and she tuned in to hear the stories on television as well. On February 12, the evening news broadcasted a tape
recording that the SLA had delivered to the Hearst family. The
recording began with Patricia's tired, flat voice saying, "Mom, Dad,
I'm okay." She said she was being kept blindfolded but was being
treated well, and she cautioned police against attempting rescue
operations that could endanger her or themselves.

The communiqué also carried the SLA's demand that the
Hearst family should give every poor person in California $70
worth of free food. Sara Jane likely watched a tired and strained
Randolph Hearst on TV, making a plea to the SLA for Patty's return. He also acknowledged the demand for food, estimating that
the cost of such a program would be $400 million, far beyond the
family's resources. Against the violent backdrop of the era, Randolph Hearst feared for his daughter's life, and he was willing to
use the family fortune to get Patty back.

Hearst said he would donate $2 million to support the People
in Need (PIN) program, which was announced on February 19,
1974. Hearst then introduced the dark-haired and intense Ludlow
Kramer, whom he had hired to direct the program. Kramer had run
a similar program in the state of Washington, where he had served
as secretary of state.

Kramer called for volunteers to help staff the food giveaway
operation. Sara Jane thought her accounting skills would most

likely be welcomed at PIN. She would offer up her talent to keep their books. Moreover, her involvement in PIN would take her away from Danville and the divorce and into the exciting, emerging world of radical politics.

No longer the Danville doctor's wife, Sara Jane was forty-four years old, smart, politically inclined, and ready to become an active participant in the dark and turbulent era that had arrived with the end of the Vietnam War. She would take PIN by storm.

Early the next morning Sara Jane drove to San Francisco. PIN's activities were staged in a hangar-sized military warehouse that Hearst had rented in China Basin, at the eastern end of the city near the docks. The large, empty, centrally located building provided a perfect space for offices and for warehousing the food they would distribute. It was conveniently located near the Oakland and San Francisco roadways for delivery trucks, and was accessible to transit hubs for the volunteers.

When she entered PIN headquarters, Sara Jane saw Kramer gathering a small group of paid and volunteer professionals to manage the PIN program. A coalition had formed to provide support personnel. This disparate group was made up of activist organizations that included the American Indian Movement, the Black Teachers Caucus, the United Methodist Church, and the United Prisoners Union. Sara Jane wanted to be sure that she got a key role within this quickly coalescing administrative structure. She glanced around, and then walked straight over to a gathering of what looked like people in charge.

"God sent me to help," Sara Jane announced, and waited for a response.

Shocked, they stopped their discussion and stared at her. When she said nothing else, they pointed her to a seat and asked her to wait until they had finished their meeting. She looked around, impressed by the activity. Phones, paper, and desk supplies that Hearst had donated to operate the program were already in full use. From this makeshift space, grocery stores, suppliers, and shipping companies were contacted to secure food for distribution. It was also the place where records of contributions would be maintained.

Sara Jane waited, listening to the steady buzz of conversation in the room, punctuated by shrieks of laughter, barked-out orders, and occasional bellows of frustration that echoed off the walls. A volunteer yelled with exasperation, as he slammed down a phone: "Shit, you'd think I was asking for something we didn't deserve!"

Sara Jane looked up at the smoglike layer that hung just below the ceiling—a heady mixture of sweat and smoke, both legal and illegal. The room crackled with energy, and the commitment of the people was palpable. Militant blacks, teenagers, pensioners, hippies, brewery workers, graduate students, architects, and society-page matrons all worked side by side. Some wore worn leather and denim vests, frayed jeans, and sandals or work boots; men and women alike had shoulder-length hair, either loose or braided. Some men, she knew, were ex-cons—hardened men unlike any she had ever met. They fascinated her.

As she waited for the meeting to end, Sara Jane carefully observed the people at the phone table. They were soliciting food donations, talking with the press, and calling organizations to recruit more volunteers. Each person at PIN had an agenda: For some, it was to feed the people; for others, it was to help free Patricia Hearst. Life here seemed to have *purpose*, in a way that none of her former lives could even touch.

Sara Jane watched the coalition volunteers at work and was impatient to join their ranks. Workers were arrayed around the horseshoe; their tabletops, lined with a bank of telephones, were strewn with paper, coffee cups, ashtrays, and doughnut boxes. These folks looked like the people she had started to get to know

when she went on marches and rallies for the United Farm
Workers.

Finally, the meeting Sara Jane had been waiting on broke up.
Peggy Maze, the assistant director Kramer had brought with him
from Washington State, walked over to Sara Jane and introduced
herself. Sara Jane immediately began telling Maze all about her accounting background. Sara Jane thought Maze seemed distracted,
but she nodded twice and said that they could really use someone
with her skills. Maze swiftly led Sara Jane over to the smallest of the
offices. The room, not much bigger than a closet, had large shelves
set up to hold accounting ledgers. Maze showed Sara Jane where all
the vendor files were located, asked her to set up books to track all
food and supplies donated to the program, and left. Maze had very
quickly and efficiently installed Sara Jane in her new office.

Peggy Maze, at thirty-six, was a crisp professional who had
devoted her life to civil service. Sara Jane saw her as a wiry, no-
nonsense person who dressed sensibly and knew her job well.
Maze generally wore a stern expression, but Sara Jane noticed that
Maze's features would occasionally soften when it was appropriate
to the task at hand—in particular, when smoothing over some hurt
caused by Kramer's rough demeanor.

Sara Jane had immediately sized Kramer up as "all business."
Most people working at PIN were slightly afraid of him. He could
be gruff, but his manner just supported his reputation as a man who
was intensely focused on getting the job done. Clearly, thought Sara
Jane, Randolph Hearst had brought in a team of people who should
be able to make the program work. She wanted to be a part of it.

Nevertheless, her poor social skills let her down again. Just as
she had failed to connect with her schoolmates or with the Danville
wives, she failed to create a rapport with the other volunteers. Sara
Jane sat silent as young, politically savvy college students told
their tales of watching Mario Savio make his legendary speech atop

a police car at UC Berkeley. Others bragged about being arrested at protests and handcuffed by the "pigs."

"It's time we made a difference," one young woman said, halting the conversation. "It's 1974 already," she complained, "and nothing has changed." Maybe, Sara Jane thought, *she* could make a difference.

SEVEN

THE ACCOUNTANT

Sara Jane threw herself passionately into the PIN food giveaway project. She wrapped herself in the ideals of PIN and made its goals her personal mission. As she walked through the warehouse, she checked all operations as though she were a supervisor.

As ever, her personal appearance mattered. She needed to look professional, even if she stood out as a beacon of white middle-class respectability in the colorful, casual, multiethnic PIN workplace. Her office "uniform" consisted of preppy navy blue slacks, a thin leather belt, and camel blazer over a crisp white blouse accented by a pearl necklace. On a chilly, rainy San Francisco day, her tan trench coat sat perched on her shoulders. She was an accountant, a professional.

In only her second week with the organization, much to the chagrin of those who worked around her, a volatile side of Sara Jane began to emerge in response to a range of organizational and operational issues.

One of the early PIN volunteers explained to me that there was a lot of tension at the warehouse, even though the atmosphere appeared relaxed. He described the scene as that of a low-level rumble of activity where workers staked out their turf and no one talked about what everyone knew was going on. Since PIN was created because of an ex-felon and leader of an organization for former convicts, it was no surprise that several prison-related gangs had shown up to run the warehouse.

There had been some fights among rival gangs, often stemming from racial or economic differences, as gang members competed for jobs. Concerned for the safety of Ludlow Kramer and others at PIN, Hearst had hired Jack Palladino, a thirty-one-year-old law student who worked for San Francisco private investigator Hal Lipset. Lipset sent Palladino to serve in a general security oversight role. He was six foot two and broad-shouldered. His responsibilities included the coordination of background checks on each employee and the supervision of security personnel hired to keep the location safe. Palladino knew that if a full-blown war broke out between the gangs there would be little he could do quickly. However, he managed to convey a strong sense of "neutrality" to the volunteers. Plus, he liked to keep people guessing about just how much control he really had. "People thought I carried a gun, and I let them think so, even though I really didn't," Palladino told me.

The PIN headquarters was essentially "controlled chaos," according to some volunteers. The distribution of food had turned into a free-for-all, and the leaders of the coalition were constantly at odds—over who was in charge, which organization was to make what decisions, and what group of volunteers would staff the seventeen Bay Area locations.

Initial implementation efforts were not meeting expectations, and the public was angry. The distribution process was erratic; there was no set schedule for the trucks, and no one seemed to know where food would be delivered on any given day. Pallets of food were disappearing from the warehouse, and some of the food donations sent to PIN never made it to the loading dock.

On February 23, 1974, the second day of food distribution, street people surrounded a food truck as it arrived at a distribution site in Richmond. The driver was a regular employee of the food company that was contributing the truckload of groceries. He pulled into his usual delivery location for this special run. Instead of finding the dock empty, he saw angry faces and clenched fists, as people screamed: "Give us our food! Open the truck! Get out! Get out! Get out!"

Fists pounded down hard on the hood of his truck as a hundred people intoned the chorus "S-L-A! S-L-A!"

At the Hunters Point location in San Francisco, an unruly mob refused to participate in the orderly distribution of the food. They rushed PIN volunteers, punching and tripping each other in order to seize their share of 150,000 pounds of fish and 820 cases of eggs.

Reports of mishaps, poor communication, violent outbursts, and missing food came in daily. Hearst told the press that he had no choice but to continue with the program as best he could, saying, "My daughter—in fact my whole family—is being held hostage."[1]

While this was going on, Sara Jane was creating her own chaos. According to Palladino, it took fewer than three weeks for her to appropriate public relations and public information responsibilities. She pushed her way into the role of de facto media liaison officer, sending out press releases and calling radio and newspapers reporters. She commandeered all of the press questions about the food distribution program; by doing so, she made the name of Sara Jane Moore well known to most of the newspaper reporters in the Bay Area. However, the challenges of press relations can be daunting for the most experienced public information officer, and Sara Jane took the problems at PIN personally.

When she arrived each day, she would go straight to her desk to see what she could do to help in some way. Most mornings she would settle into her cubicle with her back to the rest of the staff. She would huddle over her desk and ignore the activity and hullabaloo of the office and warehouse beyond it. Bent over her ledgers or her phone, her body language clearly said that she was just too busy to talk to anyone. Jack Palladino said she would frequently yelp in alarm if one of the other volunteers stopped by her office to say hello. She would throw her arms up in exasperation and berate the recalcitrant volunteer for interrupting her very important work.

According to Palladino, she would say, "You could be responsible for the demise of the entire PIN program if I don't get to complete this work on time." Her behavior was no different when Kramer or Maze came by for information.

On other days, Sara Jane's mood would be sunny. She would wander through the worktable and warehouse areas, a comrade in arms, extolling the virtues of "our" goodwill, thriving on the communal sense of purpose. It was during those perambulations that she mingled with and got to know some of the other volunteers. She seemed to be an empathetic and interested listener, a confidante of the down-and-outers, drawing out their tales of victimization by the system.

The range of volunteers was vast. There was Sue—a reed-thin woman with a ruddy complexion and a halo-shaped mop of out-of-control black hair. Sue sat nervously, almost compulsively arranging and rearranging the stacks of papers in front of her. She was twenty-eight, a member of the United Methodist Church volunteer group, and a single mother of three children, all under the age of eight. Sue complained that welfare did not give her enough money to survive. The church was providing some of her food; but without those contributed meals, she did not know how she would feed herself or her children. She wanted to go back to school, but could not afford day care.

When Sue spoke, she would look straight ahead, swallowing great gulps of air, her cloud of hair bouncing as if keeping time with her breath. She never talked about a husband or father for her children.

Then there was Jon, a political activist with the American Indian Movement (AIM). With his rounded features and dark skin, Jon appeared to be a blend of Asian and Eskimo. Stocky and broad-framed, Jon had the air of a man fighting defeat. His age was indeterminable; he might have been anywhere from twenty to forty-five. There seemed to be a constant battle between wisdom and anger in his eyes. Jon wore his long black hair in two braids tucked under the cowboy hat that he never removed, even inside PIN headquarters.

Jon lived on the Pine Ridge Indian reservation in South Dakota. He had been there for the 1973 Wounded Knee incident involving AIM activists and FBI agents.

"I got shoved around by them FBI guys many times," he told Sue and a group of volunteers assembling boxes of fruit. "They even shoved at the kids." He spoke with intensity about an incident that had taken place shortly before the major attack, when FBI agents came barging into the middle of a religious ceremony that he and other Indian friends were conducting. "We were in a sweat lodge, and them FBIs come in, they ripped open the lodge in the middle of a ceremony! And, they laughed as they did."

Even though the individual histories of the volunteers at PIN tended to be tales of victimization, the general mood was upbeat. For once, coalition members felt they were on the power team, and that they were the ones in charge.

Among the various people who fueled Sara Jane's sense that "something real is happening here" was Wilbert "Popeye" Jackson, the leader of United Prisoners Union (UPU). The charismatic and muscular forty-four-year-old black revolutionary seemed to pump adrenaline and urgency into the room with his very presence. He had spent nineteen years in and out of prison for robbery and burglary and was prone to violent rages, but he effectively masked his temper with an outwardly congenial demeanor and a soft voice. Originally from Louisiana, Jackson was an experienced informal grassroots organizer, which served him well in the haphazard PIN structure.

Sara Jane observed Popeye each time he came into the work space. He would not sit down right away. Instead, he would stand in one place and monitor the room and its inhabitants. Then, cat-like, he would prowl the perimeter before selecting his seat for the day. Sometimes he would go left, sometimes right, slowly making his way around the room, never in a rush. He would not talk to anyone on the first time around. After one full circle, when he had made his assessment, he would stop and chat with those he knew, or with those he wanted to get to know. When he finally chose a place to sit, his back was always to a wall.

Popeye noticed everyone, and he quickly learned what each person was doing. It was difficult to discern what his true intentions were.

Who was Popeye, and what was he really up to? Opinions about him varied widely. Popeye had connected with SLA leader Cinque in San Quentin. Knowing him set Popeye up with a role as the SLA's trusted and designated liaison to PIN. Others, who had also served time with Popeye, described him as a stool pigeon, a snitch, a backstabber, an opportunist, and a thug. There was some truth to both perspectives.

When the PIN program started, Popeye was out on parole. His ex-convict friends knew him and expected that he was never far from criminal activity. Prisoners Union president John Irwin told me that the police once caught Popeye selling drugs; he had hired

two young women to stand on the street in San Francisco "to en-
tice customers with their natural gifts." The two women went to
prison, but Popeye walked free. The locals simply concluded, Irwin
said, that Popeye must have been working with "the man" because
he was not "doing the time for the crime."

EIGHT

FEDERAL STRANGLEHOLD

With Popeye as her guide, Sara Jane quickly learned that paranoia among political radicals during the 1970s ran high. No one knew whether the person sitting beside them was a true believer or an imposter taking names, and those suspicions were justified. What many, including Sara Jane, were not aware of was the power of the organization that created this fear. In several instances, informants who had infiltrated political groups specifically to cause dissent and to damage the organizations' public image were caught and exposed.[1]

The organization that was acting to discredit radical groups was the Federal Bureau of Investigation (FBI), through its Counter Intelligence Program, or COINTELPRO. The program was established in 1956 under J. Edgar Hoover, the first (and, until 1972, the only) director of the FBI.

J. Edgar Hoover orchestrated thousands of systematic surveillance operations that reached into every aspect of political communities during the sixties and seventies. Almost every activist group was either infiltrated or watched. Suspicion, accusation, defensiveness, and betrayal were evident in every organization. A member accused of being an FBI informant, real or imagined, suffered instant exile from all organizations. Identification of an informant spread through the groups like wildfire.

In his early years with the FBI, Hoover directed the Bureau's attention to federal crimes, then to labor union organizers, pacifists, and "premature antifascists" in the late 1930s, to so-called subversives in government and un-Americans in general in the 1940s and 50s. Finally, in 1968, the FBI shifted its focus to what Hoover considered a new national threat—the antiwar demonstrators and left-leaning political activists. These groups were identified as the "New Left" by COINTELPRO. The FBI aggressively began to recruit civilian informants—some of whom were paid—to infiltrate organizations the FBI deemed a threat to the "national security of the country or to the stability and well-being of democracy."[2] Program activities permeated groups around the United States, with particularly focused efforts in the San Francisco Bay Area. At the time, informants delivered 83 percent of domestic intelligence gathering for the Bureau.[3] All FBI agents had the authority to determine, independently, which organizations, as well as which individuals, constituted a threat to the security of the United States.

The COINTELPRO-New Left mission initially was straightforward, if somewhat misguided: Agents were to expose, disrupt, misdirect, discredit, or otherwise neutralize the members and organizations of the radical left.[4] However, the scope of targets rapidly widened to include those groups and individuals who sought only to dissent peacefully from government policy. In practice, COINTELPRO became a dirty game as the FBI collected information on reported and rumored political views as well as the intimate details of the targets' personal lives, and then disseminated that information, true or not, in order to discredit targeted individuals in the eyes of their associates, colleagues, and families.[5]

Members of the radical and street groups who worked at PIN were quite familiar with COINTELPRO-New Left, and no one could be sure who might be an informant.

Even as the Hearst family and activist groups in the Bay Area went to work, the FBI's Criminal Justice Information Services division became involved with the Patty Hearst case, as kidnapping had long been a federal crime. The FBI did not accomplish much at first, and that lack of progress, combined with the struggle to build a massive food distribution program and the emotional strain of concern for their daughter, left the Hearsts exhausted and frustrated.

Shortly after PIN began, Hearst learned that the food he bought to give to the poor was disappearing from the loading docks at the warehouse. He requested that San Francisco police officers be stationed at PIN to watch the volunteers and that a police presence be as visible as possible. He also hired several private security agencies to fill in and begin background investigations of each of the PIN volunteers. It was through those investigations that the FBI and the San Francisco Police Department (SFPD) first heard the name Sara Jane Moore.

The SFPD and the FBI wanted to ensure that people would not take advantage of Hearst's grief by giving him false hope or phony information in exchange for money. The police also wanted to make sure that violent Black Muslims had not infiltrated the program. Hearst himself was looking to avoid theft from the program, and, of course, to open lines of inquiry that might lead to locating his daughter.

Charles Bates, the FBI agent in charge of the San Francisco office at the time, was assigned to oversee the Hearst kidnapping case. A tall, lanky man with a thick drawl, Bates was born in Louisville, Texas, and had studied political science at Southern Methodist University in Dallas. He had also earned a law degree from George Washington University in Washington, D.C. He was the same FBI agent who had handled the Watergate investigation in 1972. Bates, at fifty-four, was trim with slightly thinning salt-and-pepper hair. Those who knew him were familiar with his erect posture and his efficient, no-nonsense demeanor.

Bates did very thorough research on each person involved in PIN, as well as on all known and suspected SLA members. The influence of the FBI and the reach of the counterintelligence program were so broad, so powerful, and so exempt from oversight that no one, it seemed, was beyond surveillance.[6]

In 1972, Carl Stern was working for NBC News, analyzing and reporting on the Senate Committee on the Judiciary. Stern, now a professor of Media and Public Affairs at George Washington University, related in an interview with me[7] that he first saw a document with the title "COINTELPRO-New Left" while he was waiting to make a photocopy in a Senate office. The line for the only copy machine in an office filled with cubicles and staffers was always long, and as he and a Senate staffer were waiting, the staff member showed Stern some of the files that had been seized from an FBI office in Media, Pennsylvania. "The one that caught my eye was a directive to the resident agent to write anonymous letters to a number of Philadelphia area colleges, urging school administrators to bar SDS and similar antiwar and civil rights groups from campus," said Stern. He went on, saying, "I wondered immediately by what authority were FBI agents authorized to write anonymous letters to school administrators urging action about anything."

That marked the beginning of Stern's investigation to find out about the program. When he approached the Department of Justice and the FBI, neither would comment on COINTELPRO. Months later, Stern told me in our interview, he received a personal note from Acting FBI Director L. Patrick Gray that said, "This matter involved a highly sensitive operation. It has now been discontinued, but I do not feel that details concerning it should be released since such disclosure would definitely be harmful to the Bureau's operations and to the national security."

Stern believes that there is no way of knowing the full scope of how COINTELPRO-New Left operated and the extent to which it infiltrated people's lives. "It may have continued to be utilized and still may be," said Stern.

What we do know about the powerful effect COINTELPRO-New Left had on individuals' lives is best illustrated with two examples. The first example was the Bureau's all-out attack on civil rights leader Martin Luther King Jr. Hoover was relentless in his attacks on King, charging him with bringing a Communist influence to the civil rights movement.

On August 23, 1963, King attracted more than a quarter of a million people to the National Mall in Washington, D.C., to champion civil rights. It was at this gathering that he gave his famous "I Have a Dream" speech. This show of support for King enraged Hoover.

Following the speech, King was singled out by the FBI as "the most dangerous Negro to the future of this nation from the standpoint of Communism, the Negro and National Security."[8] Hoover approved a plan to intensify their investigative techniques on King. It was up to the FBI to mark King and bring him down on its own—to take the law into its own hands.[9] A month after King's speech, Hoover petitioned Attorney General Robert F. Kennedy to approve a wiretap on King's telephone. Kennedy agreed because he thought it would protect King.

When three civil rights workers, James Chaney, Andy Goodman, and Micky Schwerner were killed in Mississippi on June 21, 1964, King publicly questioned whether the FBI had done enough to protect the lives of civil rights activists and black citizens. This denouncement infuriated Hoover. He told reporters that King was "the most notorious liar in the country."[10]

Hoover was extremely defensive about his FBI, and to him King's criticism simply was beyond the pale. Hoover applied his "enemy to the country" label to King. The Bureau taped evidence of King's extramarital affairs and sent him a copy of the tapes with a note suggesting suicide as the only way out. In his book on the history of the FBI, Ronald Kessler detailed investigative accounts of many such FBI activities against King and others.[11]

Even after King was assassinated in Memphis on April 4, 1968, Hoover continued his campaign to discredit him and his legacy.

The second example of COINTELPRO-New Left's activities has to do with the Black Panther Party (BPP). The group was formed in Oakland, California, in the mid-1960s to promote civil rights, social welfare, and self-defense—the latter including protecting members of the black community from police brutality.

The presence of the Black Panthers was palpable in the Bay Area and across the country. Their influence could be felt in every restaurant, sidewalk, bus, and street corner they frequented. An electrical charge surrounded leaders and members alike. Leaders Huey P. Newton and Bobby Seale became legends. Small Panther cadres patrolled crime-ridden areas from the streets of Oakland to the subways in New York City; their presence was eventually welcomed by both blacks and whites traveling home from work or an evening out.

The Panthers, despite appearances, were not unitary. The extreme faction of the party viewed armed militancy as the only way to achieve liberation from white domination of blacks. The Oakland branch of the Black Panthers based their philosophy on the more violent revolutionary activist teachings of Chairman Mao; they held "study groups" in the East Bay and put their own spin on Mao's writings.

At the opposite end of the spectrum was the social service arm of the Black Panthers. It had, among other things, hired a nutritionist and created a free breakfast program in schools because the "Black Panther Party understands that our children need a nourishing breakfast every morning so that they can learn."[12] The program was so successful it at last embarrassed the federal government into creating a breakfast program in many inner-city schools around the country.

The Panthers naturally attracted the attention of the FBI, which infiltrated the organization with multiple informants. The agents worked at disrupting the organization by creating internal disputes and pitting members against one another. The Feds forged official documents to make it appear that party members had given them information, and they assigned undercover agents to engage in illegal activities that would implicate other members.

A chilling account of a COINTELPRO-New Left operation, thoroughly documented and detailed in congressional hearings, is the story of Black Panther Fred Hampton. Hampton was a charismatic leader and an effective organizer in Chicago. He set up five different breakfast programs on the West Side of Chicago, helped create a free medical center and initiated a door-to-door program of health services to test for sickle cell anemia, and promoted blood drives for the Cook County Hospital. The Chicago Black Panthers worked with local gangs to engage in some constructive community-based activities as an alternative to just protecting turf and fighting.

For Hoover, who saw the Panthers as an organization that threatened to overthrow the government of the United States, those qualities made Hampton dangerous. The FBI started a surveillance campaign focused on Hampton in 1967. Within just two years, the file had snared over four thousand pages of reports on Hampton's activities. The FBI tapped Hampton's mother's phone, and listed his name in Hoover's newly created "Agitator Index," the Bureau's file for identifying the key players in minority communities.

In 1968, the Racial Matters squad of the FBI's Chicago field office recruited William O'Neal, who had been arrested twice for interstate car theft and impersonating a federal officer. They offered O'Neal a deal: In exchange for dropping the felony charges and providing a monthly stipend, O'Neal would infiltrate the BPP as a counterintelligence operative. O'Neal joined the Panthers and quickly rose in the organization, eventually becoming director of chapter security and Hampton's bodyguard.

O'Neal was instructed to create a rift between the Party and the SDS. The Bureau released a batch of racist cartoons in the Panthers' name, aimed at alienating white activists, and launched a disinformation program to stall any projected community welfare programs sponsored by the Panthers. Bureau personnel were aiming to "destroy what the [BPP] stands for" and to "eradicate its 'serve the people' programs."[13] On July 31, 1969, the Chicago police raided and ransacked the BPP Monroe Street office, smashing typewriters, destroying food and medical supplies for the Panther health clinic and breakfast program, setting several small fires, and beating and arresting a number of Panthers for obstruction of justice.

On May 26, 1969, Hampton, who had been prosecuted for stealing $71 worth of Good Humor bars in Maywood in 1967, was sentenced to two to five years; he managed to obtain an appeal bond, and was released in August.

In early October, Hampton and his girlfriend, Deborah Johnson, pregnant with their first child, rented a small house on West Monroe Street. He was working hard to create projects to improve the image of the Black Panthers and to provide services to the community. He was invited to give a speech to the UCLA Law Students Association and was appointed to the Party's Central Committee. Hampton's chapter of BPP was recognized as the most successful chapter to offer the Serve the People program.

It was at this time that O'Neal reported to his control agent that much of the Panthers' stockpile of firearms was being stored where Hampton lived. At 4:30 A.M. on December 4, 1969, Chicago police raided Hampton's house. Hampton was shot and killed while sleeping in his bed.[14] The exact legal reason for the police raid is not clear. Chicago Police records state that it was a Black Panther attack on the police. The FBI says it "resorted to counterintelligence tactics in part because its chief officials believed that the existing law could not control the activities of certain dissident groups."[15]

The 1970s version of COINTELPRO had FBI agents and informants stalking the basements and rallies of the San Francisco Bay area, including PIN headquarters. Members of the SLA, Weather Underground, New World Liberation Front, and others were constantly on guard in case their co-workers turned out to be informants like William O'Neal.

NINE

FIRED

The photograph of Randolph Hearst on the front page of the February 20, 1974, issue of the *San Francisco Chronicle* depicts a sad and frustrated man. His gaze is downward and his face is flat, expressionless. At the time, his daughter had been held by the SLA for two weeks. The story that accompanied the photo summarized his efforts to deliver food through PIN. Hearst expressed his "frustration in trying to meet the goals of the SLA."

FBI Agent Charles Bates was equally frustrated. Bates had the uncomfortable feeling that Hearst was running his own investigation, but there was little Bates could do about it, especially with a man as powerful and wealthy as Randolph Hearst. He had asked Hearst to keep him informed of what he was trying to do on his own to find his daughter. In interviews with the press, Bates said he was concerned that Hearst was likely to get false information from profiteers, which would only frustrate him and cost him money for nothing.[1]

Bates also had his own professional view of the volunteers at PIN, and he began to reassess his strategy for gathering information that might help locate Patty Hearst. PIN was a fishbowl of information.[2] Representatives from all political organizations and points of view gathered at PIN. Information and rumor flowed freely. On several occasions, he saw Sara Jane with Popeye Jackson. As he watched their interaction, Sara Jane began to emerge as a likely candidate for a position in Bates's new army of informants.

In April, the administrative staff was closing the books on the PIN program. What had seemed like months came down to a six-week operation, from February 19 to March 25, 1974. However, recording the donations and vendors in the aftermath was a massive project.

Bates approached Sara Jane and asked her to meet with him.[3] He told her that he and his colleague would meet her on a particular street corner. His instructions, Sara Jane told me, were to "go stand on such and such a street corner and a green car with license number so-and-so will pick you up." It was like a grade B movie. On the appropriate day, she stood on the designated corner, feeling very self-conscious. A green car pulled up with Bates driving and another man in the backseat. That man, Bert Worthington, would become her control officer, the person to whom she would report.[4]

Sara Jane told me that Worthington and Bates wanted to have coffee somewhere, but she said she was frightened because their behavior had indicated it was risky for her to be seen with them. "I suggested somewhere in Golden Gate Park, but they said that it was twice as obvious to be seen sitting and talking in a car," she explained in a June 1976 *Playboy* interview. She said they ended up talking in the car in Pacific Heights.

Worthington set the stage by explaining the FBI's view of the political activists she was to report on: "Look, we need your help here. These are dangerous people. They are out to destroy the country. Many of them are dupes of foreign governments, of the KGB and the Red Chinese."

Bates gave Sara Jane a brief overview on the logistics of being an informant; she called it "Spying 101." She said he went through a long list of do's and don'ts that she could hardly follow. She said she never got the full indoctrination normally used for informants: "They wanted to get me out in the field as quickly as possible," she told me. The full program included psychological profiles of the radical left, lessons on how to identify a violent personality, and pointers on how to protect oneself from indoctrination and brainwashing. In retrospect, Sara Jane realized that a more complete briefing might have given her better defenses to deal with the political and social ideology and the seductive group dynamics of the radical movements she was about to encounter. She felt she was not properly prepared for the emotional roller coaster she went through as she began to get involved with these organizations.

The agents explained that Sara Jane's primary assignment was to get to know Popeye much better and to find out everything she could about him and his friends. The FBI hoped that Popeye could lead them to Patricia Hearst. Once regarded as a victim who needed rescue, Patty Hearst had been redefined by her own actions. In early April 1974, two months after she was kidnapped, Patty shocked the nation by participating in broad daylight in a bank robbery with the SLA. She had apparently joined the SLA—and willingly. The photo of a fully armed "Tania," as Patty had renamed herself, presented a startling contrast to her previous identity as a politically apathetic student of just a few weeks before. Patty had become a subversive and a target for the FBI.

In the car, Bates and Worthington rattled off the names of several radical groups operating in the Bay Area. Some of these groups were well known to Sara Jane; others she had never heard of before. They wanted her to begin attending these organizations' meetings and to take notes, they told her. She should then write down the names of people she knew there and try to get the names and addresses of others from sign-up sheets. She would also attend study groups—which, the agents said, generally encompassed both political education and a cover for revolutionary planning—to find out both who was participating in them and what plans were being made.

The agents told Sara Jane to watch for signs of divisiveness within the groups. As she put it, "the Feds" always liked to know who was becoming angry within the organizations because that might offer an opening for them to infiltrate and crush the group. They trained FBI informants to seek to gain ground with an angry or unhappy person by taking his side, building trust, and gradually becoming a conduit of inside information.

Bates explained how the information feeds would work; Sara Jane could communicate with the FBI in three ways: in writing, on tape, or in person. She would write reports to a fictitious company, naming suspicious people, and include herself on the list. Then she would sign the reports with a code name and mail them to a post office box. When she would make reports on audiotape, she would be told where to drop the tapes; the drop site would be a different place each time. If personal visits with her handler, Worthington, were deemed necessary, they would never meet at FBI headquarters. The location for the meeting would be designated by the FBI and communicated to her. Worthington told her never to use her phone at home to contact the FBI, but instead to call him from pay phones at least once a week—more often if she had particular news. They agreed that Sara Jane would be reimbursed for her expenses.[5]

When they were finished, Worthington drove her back to PIN headquarters. Sara Jane asked her final question: "How should I behave?"

"Just be yourself," Worthington said.

Popeye became her first target. She needed to come up with a reason to reconnect with him, and was trying to work out that approach. One day Randolph Hearst was meeting with Ludlow Kramer at PIN. It had been two months since Patty Hearst had been taken captive, and Randolph Hearst was desperate.

Randolph had kept his composure throughout the press conferences and media demands. He quietly met with anyone offering information about his daughter. In an effort to control rumors, he told editors at his paper to play down the story.[6]

Hearst was observant and paid attention to the people who hung around the warehouse. He had seen Sara Jane interact with volunteers as she went about her accounting duties.[7] After a couple of weeks, Hearst approached Sara Jane and asked if she had heard anything of note recently. She told me he said he believed that she was very well-connected to the political communities through the contacts she had made at PIN. He told her that he hoped that she could develop secret lines of communication between the Hearsts and the SLA. She said she would do what she could to help, and immediately began working on a strategy to gain information.

Unfortunately, however, Sara Jane had been slowly alienating the staff at PIN. Jack Palladino, the security agent hired by Hearst, said people had complained to him about Sara Jane's behavior. He told me she angered many of the staff with her loud complaints about how much work she had to do, and that they were interfering with her concentration. Sara Jane's behavior continued to waver between sweetly complimenting volunteers for efficient distribution of the canned goods and screaming because someone had interrupted her train of thought by asking a question.

A week after Sara Jane's indoctrination as an informant there was a confrontation at PIN. As she entered the warehouse and turned in the direction of her office, she stopped dead in her tracks. Jack Palladino and several volunteers were crowded around her desk thumbing through the pages of her accounting ledgers.

"What are you doing?" she shouted.

Palladino said Sara Jane charged toward her desk, wild with indignation that anyone would dare to touch her books. Without breaking her stride, she grabbed the ledgers. "No one touches my ledgers except me. If there is any checking to do, I'll do it. Now get the hell out of here!"

Throughout the PIN operation, Palladino said, Sara Jane had consistently refused to give any information to Kramer or Maze about accounts receivable or payable. She had prepared no summary reports of donations, inventory, or distributions at PIN. Palladino told me she had ignored requests for such reports or had met them with a standard shouted response: "You're hindering my work—I'll have that tomorrow. Stop interrupting me."

"They were not afraid she was going to be violent," Palladino said. "She just screamed a lot and intimidated all these really nice people." However, Palladino was not taking any chances. Quickly and efficiently, he and another security guard each grabbed Sara Jane under one arm, while a third gathered her purse and coat. The two men propelled her out of her office and through the front door of PIN headquarters in one swift movement.

"What are you doing?" she asked, startled.

"It's time for you to leave, Sara Jane," said Palladino. "Your services are no longer required here, per Mr. Kramer and Ms. Maze."

"But I'm the chief bookkeeper!" she protested. "No one knows how to do anything here; they're just a bunch of idiots!"

Palladino and other security guards ignored her comments and continued to drag her screaming toward her car. "You can't run this place without me! You need me here! You people are worthless; no one is as dedicated as I am."

"Go home, Sara Jane," said Palladino. "Get some rest. And don't come back here. You will not be let back in."

Palladino told me that on the same day Sara Jane was fired, he had received the results of the security inquiry that he had initiated on her when she first volunteered. "The investigation I ran on her found she had given a phony address in Danville, a phony Social Security number, a phony work history. I wasn't even sure she gave us her right name," Palladino said.

With Sara Jane off the premises, Palladino said another volunteer with accounting experience went into the office and pulled open the desk drawer. Her jaw dropped as she found checks that had not been deposited, a host of unpaid vendors' invoices crinkled and stuffed in the back of the drawer, and bills of lading for shipments received that had never been entered or receipted.

Sara Jane once told me that she never looks back. After her unceremonious ejection from PIN, she simply reset her strategy and came roaring back out into the world. Her control agent had warned her that people even suspected of squealing (passing information along to the federal government) could consider their lives in jeopardy. Neither Hearst nor the FBI told the other that they had enlisted Sara Jane Moore as an informant, and Sara Jane did not tell them either.

Desperate to get his daughter back, Hearst was working every avenue and every angle. He saw a unique opportunity arise. Popeye Jackson—the so-called designated liaison to PIN for the SLA—was coming up for a hearing on a parole violation. He was in need of any help he could get to influence the parole board in his favor. Hearst was impressed with Popeye, one of the few people in PIN who could get the volunteers organized and moving into coordinated action. In fact, Popeye had helped keep the program from turning into total anarchy.

Popeye, in turn, was impressed with Hearst. While other high-level PIN executives were lounging over fancy dinners at Victor's in the St. Francis Hotel each evening after work, Hearst was willing to go anywhere and to work with anyone who could help, regardless of background or social class. The attention and approval of this rich and important man stoked Popeye's ego. Popeye told his friends, "Hearst has great respect for me as a man, and I respect him."

The two men met and talked, and Hearst directed his newspaper, *The San Francisco Examiner*, to give Popeye's community work favorable publicity—quite the opposite of the position that the staunchly conservative daily would normally have taken toward a parole violator. On April 7, 1974, an *Examiner* story reported on Popeye's efforts to curb recidivism among ex-cons by way of the literacy program he developed and ran. That was followed two days later by an editorial that urged the state parole board to keep Popeye on the streets so that he could continue his work. Two weeks later, the parole board did so.

Hearst revealed in interviews that he had not expected Popeye to be moved by the pain of this father whose daughter had been kidnapped. He did, however, hope that in return for the favors he had done for Popeye, the ex-con would reciprocate by sharing any information he received about where Patty was being held. When no such information was forthcoming, and PIN was shut down, Hearst pinned some of his hopes on the possibility that Sara Jane might be able to get information from Popeye.[8]

Sara Jane was eager to start gathering information, and she came up with the perfect cover. She asked Popeye to be her political mentor and teach her about the various organizations in San Francisco.[9] That initial contact soon grew into something of a friendship, and that spring Sara Jane could often be seen hanging out with Popeye and his followers in San Francisco's multiethnic Mission District. She spent a lot of time in the Mission Street cafés, about as far from Danville's upscale restaurant scene as she could get.

Sara Jane turned out to be a natural at ingratiating herself. Whenever she left Danville for the city to hang out with Popeye's crowd, she would stuff an extra pack or two of cigarettes in her purse. She knew that he and his cronies would bum smokes from her as they drank coffee from ceramic mugs and talked for hours. The cigarettes were just part of her dues for membership in the group.

Although she was not learning anything about where Patty Hearst was being held, Sara Jane was learning a lot about Popeye. He claimed that he was an equal-opportunity political liberal. As she watched him in action, however, she did not believe a word of it. She knew she was being jived and charmed. Every word out of his mouth was canned, as though he were reading a script. She did, however, develop respect for Popeye's well-regarded recidivism prevention program, and she believed that he really was trying to make a difference in the lives of ex-cons.

TEN

THE SPY

The UPU headquarters, a storefront on Twenty-fourth Street in San Francisco, was Sara Jane's home base as she began her surveillance activities of the radical underground for the FBI. An oversize couch served as a temporary bed when not in use as seating space for the self-help groups that met there. On the back wall hung a poster of Nelson Rockefeller, wanted for "Lies, Conspiracy, Armed Robbery and Murder." Below Rockefeller hung a recruiting notice that urged members to "Support the Black Liberation Army," depicting a smiling soldier with a rifle.[1]

Even the less militant groups at that time were more potentially dangerous for an informant than the peaceful protestors who marched with César Chávez in 1973 to support the farm workers. In a letter to me, Sara Jane said that moving into these radical groups was a dizzying assignment. In the beginning, she was uncomfortable mingling with some of the people.

She began her infiltration activities in April 1974 by dropping in at the UPU offices for half days. Ostensibly, she was there to help the UPU, but her primary goal was to keep her eyes and ears wide open on Popeye's home turf, to learn what she could about him and those around him for her FBI reports.

While spying for the FBI, Sara Jane carried a message to Popeye from Hearst in May 1974: In exchange for information on
Patty, Hearst would pay for Popeye's son to attend a prestigious
private school. Popeye did not offer any information, and no money
ever changed hands. Nothing more was ever said about this offer,
and Popeye and Sara Jane continued to interact casually on a personal level.

Popeye told Sara Jane about a newly forming political study
group in San Francisco starting that May, and she eagerly agreed
to attend. She recognized that this activity would provide an additional opportunity to infiltrate the radical movement more deeply,
and, now that spying for the FBI was her only occupation, she
threw herself into it fully.

Sara Jane joined the study group with her characteristic enthusiasm. The curriculum for the group consisted of books on the lives
and writings of Karl Marx, V. I. Lenin, and Mao Zedong, who were
considered the founders of socialist political action and organization. She was still living in her spacious home in Danville, and the
commute could sometimes take two hours each way.

The study group met on Tuesday nights at 7:00 P.M. in the
basement of the church at Sixteenth Street and Dolores Street, in
the heart of San Francisco's Mission District. When Sara Jane
walked downstairs and into her first meeting, she found herself in
an airless room that smelled of mold and was crowded with just
fourteen people. Sara Jane brought her ardent interest in all
things political and inserted herself into the intense small-group
discussions.

Ever the good student, Sara Jane wrote down the names of
everyone in attendance, as she had been instructed to do, trying
not to be too obvious about it. As everyone took notes at these
meetings, no one paid any attention to her jottings. Sara Jane listened attentively to the group leader, a nervous, twitchy woman
who explained that she had been fired from her job at San Fran-

cisco State University four years earlier for setting an American flag on fire. Some in the audience nodded approvingly while others rolled their eyes. Sara Jane wrote it all down.

As the meeting wore on, she realized that these people were serious. This was not like a suburban social group in which members would end the evening discussing art galleries or vacation resorts; nor was it a mere exercise in pure intellectualism. Rather, it was a group of well-spoken and well-read people—whites, blacks, and Latinos together—strongly intent on social change. In a letter to me, she wrote that it was at this point that she truly began to pay attention to what they were saying.

Behind the rhetoric, the basic message of the evening was fundamental socialism, with a very strong activist component. They discussed the Socialist Workers Party mission statements and issues such as "Living under domination and struggling against it exacts a personal toll. Socialists regard the distortion of personal life and interpersonal relations under capitalism as a political matter. Although workers create society's wealth, they have no control over its production and distribution."[2]

Sara Jane came to believe that these people were sincere. "These were dedicated people looking for qualitative change," she wrote in a letter to me. None of what she heard sounded crazy to her. In fact, it made sense; a lot of sense.

Only Sara Jane knew what had evolved in her past. In her mind, she felt victimized, and this would have made her sympathetic to the party principles. Within the past couple of years she'd lost her marriage, she was about to lose her home, and she'd been singled out by the folks at PIN. Sara Jane had the tools and understanding needed to stand up for those who were less able to fight the unfairness in the system. She shared some of these feelings with the group and stressed her own commitment to the radical cause.

Although she was beginning to agree with the people she was reporting on, Sara Jane stuck to her job as a government informant.

She worked hard to blend in and gain the radicals' approval. She watched to see who seemed angry, who was frustrated, who was ready for action, who did not pay much attention to what was being said, and she included all of that information in her reports to the FBI.[3]

On May 16, 1974, things heated up around the Patty Hearst kidnapping. "Tania" had fired twenty-seven shots from a semiautomatic shotgun at the façade of Mel's Sporting Goods in San Francisco to provide cover for two of her kidnappers, Bill and Emily Harris, who were attempting to steal ammunition inside. The three escaped.

The following day, May 17, Sara Jane met Worthington at the Bicycle Café, an Italian restaurant on Columbus Street in North Beach, for her first in-person report to the FBI. The older beatniks and young hippies who haunted this bohemian neighborhood of poetry bookshops and espresso bars would have been stunned to learn that the unimposing man and woman seated there were discussing FBI business.

Sara Jane was excited. The study group had already met twice, and she had a lot to report. She told Worthington about the Marx and Lenin classes, gave him an updated list of names of the people who attended, and told him what she knew about each one. Worthington thought she was doing a great job. Clearly, this group was a perfect venue for her to meet people who were involved in local radical politics.[4]

One woman Sara Jane described in detail in her report was Camilla Hall. Hall was friends with Bill and Emily Harris, Patty's kidnappers.

Sara Jane knew that Hall was connected with the SLA— apparently brought in by her lover, Patricia Soltysik, known as "Mizmoon." Worthington described Hall as a warrior. She had worked as a gardener in the East Bay Regional Park District, but had recently been fired, despite her stellar job performance, because she was a vocal union activist. Still, with her warm smile and bib overalls, she seemed more like a flower child to Sara Jane than the warrior type Worthington perceived her to be.[5]

Sara Jane also told Worthington that Hearst had asked her to help him find his daughter. She explained that Hearst was feeling desperate; he had said he had the resources to get the help he needed. She explained that Hearst believed she had contacts and might be able to provide information.[6]

Worthington listened to her reports on how and why Hearst had given Popeye the favorable write-up and editorial in *The Examiner*. This meant Hearst was running his own private search in parallel with FBI efforts, brokering deals with marginalized individuals and buying his own informants. Worthington did not like it, but there was no real way the Bureau could stop a man as powerful as Randolph Hearst. Moreover, as it was FBI policy not to disclose its sources, they could not even tell Hearst that Moore was also working for them.[7]

Bates was unsure who would resolve the kidnapping—Hearst or the FBI. If anything went wrong with or as a result of Hearst's efforts, the FBI would surely be blamed, even if it was because Hearst had gotten in the way. FBI Director Clarence Kelley ordered the team to apply every possible resource to the Hearst case and solve it.[8]

On May 18, Sara Jane turned on the TV to see a major SLA story breaking. Acting on an anonymous tip, four hundred Los Angeles police officers, accompanied by members of the FBI, the California Highway Patrol, and the Los Angeles Fire Department, had surrounded a suspected SLA safe house on East Fifty-fourth Street, in a black neighborhood.[9]

"Come out with your hands up!" they commanded over a bullhorn.

The front door opened and a small boy, Tony Lewis, age eight, walked out. He didn't understand what he heard and said later he came outside from his home to see what the noise was about. When he saw the police and guns he began to cry and call for his mother, Minni, who was passed out on her bed inside the house from pills and alcohol.[10]

After Tony calmed down, he told the detectives that there were people inside with guns. The SWAT team called again for the occupants to come out. The front door slowly opened and a tall, thin man named Clarence Ross emerged. He clasped his hands behind his head and walked toward the police. When he was questioned about the other occupants in the house, he told a very different story. He denied that anyone was inside with guns. He said only the owner, Minni Lewis, was inside, asleep. There was never an explanation why Ross was in the home or what his connection was to the SLA.[11]

After the police made several unsuccessful attempts to persuade those inside to come out, the SWAT team fired tear gas projectiles into the house. The people inside the house responded with heavy bursts of automatic gunfire.

The battle had begun.

For the next two hours, bullets flew back and forth in what seemed to be a standoff. Then, suddenly, the house caught fire.

Over a loudspeaker, the police issued an order: "Come on out! The house is on fire! You will not be harmed!"

Two women—neither of them SLA members, as it later turned out—left from the rear of the house, and one came out the front. Then Camilla Hall and Patty Soltysik ran out of the house as well, firing their weapons at the police. They were shot dead on the spot. Sara Jane realized that Worthington knew what he was talking about when he called Camilla Hall a warrior.

Eventually, the fire department put out the blaze. Inside, police found the bullet-riddled bodies of SLA members Nancy Ling Perry, Angela Atwood, William Wolfe, and Donald DeFreeze—the notorious Cinque. By this time, large crowds had gathered in the neighborhood to watch the battle, and millions more were watching on national television.

The back of the SLA was broken by the Los Angeles shoot-out, but the FBI still had not found Patty Hearst.

Sara Jane was shocked by these events. She was familiar with many of the SLA members who had been killed. She wrote to me that when she next met with Worthington, she told him that she sensed some distance, and that she did not feel as close to Popeye as she had earlier. Worthington replied that Popeye really didn't matter anymore, but it would be good for Sara Jane to simply stay on speaking terms with him, because there was someone else, someone far more important, whom she needed to focus on. Apparently, Popeye had simply been a training prop for Sara Jane. The FBI had used her relationship with Popeye to prepare her to infiltrate the work of someone they considered to be much more critical.

Sara Jane would only identify her next FBI target by the pseudonym "Tom." She had come to know him over the preceding couple of years as they worked together on such political and social issues as feeding the hungry and gaining farm workers' rights. The FBI had not been successful in getting any other informant close to Tom, and they hoped to break through with Sara Jane. The FBI labeled Tom a major leftist anti-imperialist revolutionary. Knowing that Sara Jane, who now had some field experience, was his friend, the FBI planned to exploit the situation as much as they could.[12]

Who was Tom? Sara Jane would only say that he was important in the radical movement, had recruited key people to it, and that although he supported militant guerrilla activities he did not build or set bombs. Whoever he was, by late May 1974, Sara Jane began spending more and more time with him, and she included his activities in her reports to the FBI.

In the meantime, Sara Jane continued to attend the study groups. She was spending a lot of time with people in the radical community, and they were feeding her ego. She told me she had good relationships with these people. She also liked the attention they paid to her. They were her family now. It seemed that she had found a new home within a community whose mission struck a chord with her.

The only sour note for Sara Jane was the grinding commute between Danville and San Francisco. She was being worn down driving back and forth at all hours, and she also had to juggle the logistics and expenses of Frederic's care, since he frequently stayed overnight at the Palmer School.

In June 1974, the decision to move was made for her: Her marriage had been annulled, and the house was in foreclosure. She decided that she would go to San Francisco, where people liked and respected her. She gathered up eight-year-old Frederic and all their belongings and moved to a rented apartment at 565 Guerrero Street. She loved being in her own place and sharing it with her son. She was certain she would feel at home in this historic urban neighborhood.

ELEVEN

THE MISSION

Sara Jane's modest apartment represented her new life. It was completely different from life in Danville, and that was just fine with her. The sunny, low-rent neighborhood, just southwest of downtown San Francisco, was replete with old two-family Victorian homes, squeezed together side by side. Most had not seen a fresh coat of paint in fifteen years. The air was filled with the sound of people speaking Spanish and the aroma of exotic food.

To a casual observer, Sara Jane, who still dressed like a preppy suburban mom, must have looked out of place in this community of recent immigrants, college students, and struggling blue-collar families. For her, however, the Mission was a fit; it offered a freedom she had not known for years. Here she could find all the comforts of home: a dry cleaner who pressed clothes to her satisfaction; a fruit stand with firm mangos and crisp apples; and a bakery with wonderful smells where she could pick up milk along with fresh-baked breads. She found cheap but decent neighborhood cafés and coffee shops that served meals on thick earthenware plates, like the Delrina on Guerrero Street, one haunt of movement folks, and the Dolores Café on Dolores Street.

She soon found work at a local mom-and-pop linoleum flooring store, where she earned enough to pay for rent and food. The job made few demands on her mind, and none at all on her time outside normal working hours. She had established the dream life of a San Francisco radical.

The only imperfections in this perfect life were the difficulties Sara Jane encountered in trying to break into some of the political groups on the extensive list assigned to her by the FBI. She found some of the groups on the FBI list to be very loosely organized, without regular meeting times; a few were little more than a name and a vague concept with no clear vision or structure. Those that were well organized were reticent about giving out their meeting locations. Often she learned nothing more than the names of the groups. Paranoia and suspicion among radical organizations arose from stories of informants being revealed and the obvious presence of agents.

If Sara Jane did manage to pierce the wall of suspicion, she would immediately offer her accounting skills; sometimes that tactic helped, but not always. She did, however, gradually become a member of a number of the better-organized groups.

In early July 1974, as Sara Jane spent more time with Popeye to review and discuss the class she was taking, she found that his poorly masked chauvinism grated on her sensitivities.[1] At some point early in their relationship, Popeye had borrowed money from Sara Jane. Sara also often lent Popeye her 1970 Toyota when he needed "wheels."[2] A member of UPU said Popeye returned her car slightly damaged on one occasion, and didn't recall the car ever being repaired. Their relationship, which had been unraveling, was now torn beyond reconciliation.[3]

"He treated people like shit," Sara Jane said in a *Berkeley Barb* interview. "He wanted money and a middle-class life. He did not give people the same respect he expected from them."[4] People in Sara Jane's circle at the time had a slightly different perspective on what happened.

Persons quoted in articles published in the *Berkeley Barb* and in the *San Francisco Chronicle* claimed that Sara Jane had been physically attracted to Popeye, but the feeling was not mutual. These observers were convinced that his lack of interest in her was a contributing factor to her cooling to him.[5]

If her romantic life was not going well, her efforts as an informant were being appreciated. She was promoted by the FBI from informant to PSI—a potential security informant.

Her success as an informant, however, began to make her uneasy. In her June 1976 *Playboy* interview, Sara Jane said that in July 1974 she decided she could no longer report on friends like Tom and others who had invited her into their circles. She could not continue to be a snitch.

She made the decision to come clean by "outing" herself to Tom, who was ostensibly her number-one target. She invited Tom to her apartment, and, according to her interview with *Playboy*, the following occurred:

> I was just talking to him and then I said, "There is something I've got to tell you." Finally, I said, "I'm a pig."
> He said, "SFPD?" I said, "No."
> He said, "State?" I said, "No."
> He said, "Treasury Department?" I said, "No."
> He said, "That leaves only one. FBI?" I said, "Yes."
> He didn't believe it. That is why I was so good at it. I don't look like an agent. I'm a white, upper-middle-class suburbanite wandering around in the left.
> But he asked me enough questions to satisfy himself and finally he realized that I was, indeed what I said I was.

Sara Jane said Tom told her to make her own way without the FBI, to rely on her own two feet only. It was likely that Tom was telling Sara Jane to leave the informant life behind. He said he would keep her secret as long as she never revealed his true identity to anyone. Sara Jane agreed to the deal. After that conversation, Tom kept his distance from her.

But by then Sara Jane's role as informant had spread beyond the FBI. Building upon her contacts with Bureau agents and their knowledge of her radical contacts, other law enforcement agencies had begun to ask for her assistance. These included both the SFPD, where Inspector Jack O'Shea was her primary contact, and the weapons division of the Federal Bureau of Alcohol, Tobacco, and Firearms (ATF).

Sara Jane had great difficulty keeping a low profile that August, and she was feeling isolated and alone. Her FBI control agent, Worthington, was on temporary assignment in Washington for more than a month that summer, and was unaware of how her position had changed. When he returned to San Francisco in September, Sara Jane told him that she had blown her cover to Tom. She believed other groups had not fully accepted her, and that they were growing suspicious of her. Sara Jane told me Worthington was disgusted by her behavior, but kept his cool. He reacted with thinly veiled annoyance, immediately dropped her as a source, and strongly advised her to get out of the movement for her own good.

Sara Jane didn't take Worthington's advice. She had made too many contacts and, despite the suspicions circulating, she felt she had created a context for herself. There was no way she would give up her newfound standing in San Francisco's radical society. Instead, she continued to attend movement meetings, to maintain and extend her contacts, and even to make important new ones. Her commitment to radical causes continued to grow.

As September passed for Sara Jane without FBI support, she finally realized the powerful role the agency had played in her life. She felt their absence deeply. "When they cut you off," she lamented to me, "you're really cut off."

"Being out of touch with the FBI made me realize to what extent my studies had been directed by them," Sara Jane said in that same conversation, "and that it was from them I was learning who was doing what on the left."

In October she approached the FBI again, and she was pleasantly surprised that they agreed to reinstate her as an informant. According to Sara Jane, it was the first time the Bureau had ever continued with a blown source. She was proud to be back on their list.

Among the radical groups that would figure strongly in Sara Jane's activities over the next year, now that she was an informant again, were Prairie Fire, Vietnam Veterans Against the War/Winter Soldier Organization (VVAW), and Tribal Thumb.

Prairie Fire grew out of the student movements of the 1960s and the Weather Underground; it focused on racism, black liberation, and the welfare of the Vietnamese people. Early in 1974, the Weather Underground published *Prairie Fire: The Politics of Revolutionary Anti-Imperialism,* and discussion groups rapidly sprang up in cities around the country. These groups came together to form the Prairie Fire Organizing Committee (PFOC). The group's charter was aimed at the support of oppressed peoples in their struggles against injustice and it declared itself to be against all U.S. imperialism.

The Vietnam Veterans Against the War group emerged, as the name suggests, among returning Vietnam vets who were disaffected both by the war and by the ways in which they were—or were not—welcomed upon their return. They focused primarily on political approaches to social change, starting with attempts to educate the public on the negative aspects of the war they had fought in Vietnam. The group developed into a national veterans' organization that campaigned for peace, justice, and the rights of all U.S. veterans. As a group that was against the war that the Washington establishment favored, the VVAW was a highly visible target for COINTELPRO-New Left.

Tribal Thumb, the third of these organizations, was one of the least-known radical groups. The creator and motivator of Tribal Thumb was Earl Satcher, who had been sentenced to five years in prison for aggravated assault. While serving that sentence at Soledad Prison, Satcher spent time with George Jackson, who later was killed while allegedly trying to escape from San Quentin.

Satcher was charismatic in a rough-hewn way. He was prison strong, but he was also philosophical and intellectually curious. Although he had only a high school education, he had used his time at Soledad to read Mao's writings and to study Jackson's interpretations.

Back out on the street, Satcher founded Tribal Thumb, first as a prisoners' rights organization to compete with the already popular Prisoners Union run by John Irwin,[6] an ex-con who would eventually earn a doctorate in sociology with a focus on criminal justice, and its spin-off organization, the UPU, headed by Popeye Jackson.

Publicly, Tribal Thumb's objective was to reform the prison system and bring attention to repressive government laws. The group around Satcher operated out of an office at Kenyatta College, which was renamed Cañada College and is still located in Redwood City. (The college was known as Kenyatta College to the African American population, in honor of the Kikuyu leader Jomo Kenyatta, and as Cañada College to Latinos.) Satcher worked with students there on a prison project.

While many of the left-leaning groups did genuine community work, the office at Kenyatta was more of a front for Satcher, a means to provide a public relations image that would help him avoid legal charges for his underground activities.

Satcher believed in diversification of assets, and he involved himself and his organization in many—and varied—endeavors.

One of those was an organized food cooperative. The food distribution program was divided into two parts: One was Wellspring Reunion, which maintained a ranch and distributed food in Honey Dew, near Eureka, California, about 275 miles north of San Francisco. Wellspring also had a small restaurant in San Francisco. The second and much larger part of the operation was the People's Food System,[7] on Folsom Street, part of a network of food stores. A great volume of food passed through the stores every day. A lot of money was changing hands in the system, and that attracted Satcher.

Marie Ferreboeuf, a member of the Wellspring Reunion in 1974 and now an attorney in San Francisco, told me that Satcher would go to the Wellspring restaurant often and to the ranch, which served as a retreat for Tribal Thumb members, for several days at a time.[8] According to Ferreboeuf, it was an idyllic retreat; people from the restaurant would go there and stay. No one ever knew who was working at the restaurant at any given time, and no one was really in charge. "It was a very passive place after a while," she said. "We read philosophy, Mao, talked politics, but views were varied. A lot of people were just passing through."

A tranquil ranch seemed like an odd setting for the activities of the leader of a prison reform group with a reputation for being tough, but Ferreboeuf disagrees. "Earl was very charming to everyone there," she recalled. "He was interested in a lot of things and quite open-minded." The ranch offered a quiet, green environment, a place where people could get away from the city. No one raised their voices; there was no conflict. It was an open, polygamous community. She said Satcher mentioned buying the restaurant as a side business, for a way to have cash available when he needed it.

Within the communities of the left in the 1970s, shared food programs, or cooperatives, were a popular concept. Neighbors often pooled resources to purchase food directly from farmers and small distributors. Groups would create a phone list to find available goods. A few people would take orders from all of the neighbors, and volunteers would then take the list and buy from the farmer's markets. The goal was to create orders large enough to enable the group to buy directly and therefore more economically.

It was this system that Satcher wanted to penetrate. Beyond purchasing food, Satcher sought the opportunity to gain a board position within the collective, another way of gaining control over the money coming into the system.[9]

Ferreboeuf said that Satcher was well known among the food collectives in San Francisco. His attitude on the street was very different from his demeanor at the ranch; in San Francisco he was far from mellow. Some of the other food collective members saw Satcher as the cult leader of the Wellspring group.[10]

Members of Tribal Thumb kept to themselves. Ultimately, however, in the summer of 1975, Sara Jane was able to establish contact and then a connection with this shadowy organization. That she accomplished this is a testament to the skills she had developed. She became friendly enough with one woman in Tribal Thumb for them to become roommates for several weeks that summer. This woman's identity has never been revealed.[11]

Kahn Family at Olaf Kahn's funeral, in 1965, including Sara Jane's brothers and sister, and three of Sara Jane's children. Sara Jane was not at the funeral.

Sara Jane Moore Senior Picture. Stonewall Jackson High School, Charleston, West Virginia, Class of 1947

Sara Jane Moore Spanish Club high school picture. Stonewall Jackson High School, Charleston, West Virginia, Class of 1947

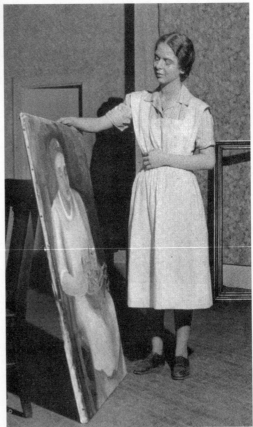

Sara Jane Moore Thespians high school senior play, playing the role of Abby in "The Late Christopher Bean." Stonewall Jackson High School, Charleston, West Virginia, Class of 1947

Charles Bates, Agent in Charge of San Francisco FBI Office in 1975, recruited Sara Jane Moore as an FBI informant.

Ludlow Kramer, Director of the PIN program, recruited by Randolph Hearst after successfully managing a similar program as Secretary of State in Washington State.

Peggy Maze, Assistant to Ludlow Kramer and manager of the day-to-day operations of PIN, directing activity at the PIN calling center.

People began lining up before dawn on March 5 for the third distribution of free food, which Randolph Hearst hoped would win his daughter's freedom. This line was almost 250 strong at sunrise at San Francisco's Grove Street distribution center.

Patty Singer, volunteer tutor and Popeye's girlfriend, shown at United Prisoners Union headquarters, holding her son by Popeye Jackson. A poster of Vice President Rockefeller as a "Wanted" criminal can be seen in the background.

Willard "Popeye" Jackson, leader of the United Prisoners Union, active in PIN, and Sara Jane's link and mentor in the radical underground.

President Gerald Ford emerging from the St. Francis Hotel and wading into the crowd to greet the citizenry.

*Sara Jane Moore being carried away from the scene of the attempted assassination by SFPD officers and Secret Servicemen (her boots are visible at the left).*

Sara Jane, 49, seemed cheerful and confident from her hospital bed at the Federal Correctional Institution in Lexington, Kentucky on September 28, 1979 after her six-week hunger strike. Moore was transferred from Alderson, where she demanded changes in the prison isolation rules.

Sara Jane Moore, June 1975, interviewing for the Berkely Barb.

Sara Jane Moore in a holding cell in San Francisco, awaiting her hearing in December 1975.

Judge Samuel Conti, federal judge who conducted Sara Jane Moore's trial/hearing in October 1975– January 1976.

TWELVE

DOUBLING

In the fall of 1974, the East Bay chapter of Prairie Fire wanted to reprint and locally distribute copies of their book *Prairie Fire: The Politics of Revolutionary Anti-Imperialism* to encourage and support study groups. They needed $10,000 to cover printing costs, and that was a problem. The revolutionaries did not have the money; they did not charge membership dues, and they did not run bake sales. Neither did they have anything to put up for collateral to secure a traditional loan.

The situation seemed a perfect fit with the imperative given to Sara Jane by the FBI: to find and exploit organizational vulnerability. The Bureau had agreed to provide Sara Jane with money for loans, or to make equipment available if that could get them information. Sara Jane's job was to become trusted enough within an organization to broker a deal—without, of course, revealing the source of the funds.

Even in this vacuum, Sara Jane could not make any headway with Prairie Fire. She told them that she had found a way to obtain a loan to reprint the book, and that she had a printer arranged, but in return they had to give her the original printing plates.[1] Prairie Fire said they did not want her help.

In the meantime, Sara Jane also attempted to infiltrate the East Bay chapter of the VVAW. During her first couple of meetings in the fall of 1974, she mistook the casual atmosphere to mean that it was a laid-back organization. But these were, in fact, battle-scarred soldiers. Although it had been easy for her in the past to walk into a group and begin talking to people, the vets had learned not to trust anybody.

Sara Jane offered to help VVAW organize their extended membership list, which they had been talking about doing. Ever suspicious of newcomers, they stalled Sara Jane for over a month before letting her into their systems at all.[2]

Shortly after that happened, the chapter president received a phone call from a member in another VVAW chapter. The caller said that he knew that Sara Jane had infiltrated the VVAW East Bay chapter, that she was known to ask too many questions in a number of other movement groups, and that she was reputed to be an FBI informant. Given that alert, and a description confirming the behavior pattern they had observed, the VVAW leadership decided to do their own investigation of Sara Jane.[3]

The VVAW talked to a number of radical leaders in the Bay Area, including Popeye Jackson. Popeye told them the story about Sara Jane carrying the message that Hearst would pay for Popeye's son to go to school in exchange for SLA information. Popeye told them he had refused the money and had given her no information. He told the VVAW that he had begun to grow more and more suspicious that "Sara Jane was not only a lackey for Hearst, but . . . that she worked for the FBI."[4]

Later that year, Mark Bramhill, a member of the VVAW steering committee would say in a letter to the *Berkeley Barb* that Sara Jane "volunteered information she found about our addresses, jobs and some organizational affiliations but never once, until confronted with concrete evidence, did she admit to being an FBI informer. She did not bring up allegations against Popeye Jackson, but she did try to refute the allegations that Popeye had brought up about her offering him money."[5]

Sara Jane was voted out of the VVAW.

It never occurred to Sara Jane that Worthington might keep up with the activities of Prairie Fire and the VVAW. He was aware of her failures with those groups. As she told me later, the FBI had informants everywhere.

Once again, Sara Jane had to regroup and put her less-than-successful efforts behind her. She did not analyze what had happened in these groups or think about what she could have done differently; she just decided to redouble her efforts to stay in the good graces of the radical movement.

Sara Jane's life now took an odd turn, or, perhaps, an odd split. In the beginning, she had idealized her FBI work and saw informing on the radical left as work for the greater good. But the deeper she went, the more she found herself agreeing with the movement's agendas.

She continued to report on people and events of the radical left to the FBI. She also began to draw actively from her sources in order to gather data on Bureau activities that she could share with the radicals. She was truly "doubling"—serving as an information gatherer and reporter for both sides.

Sara Jane learned that many members of the radical movements were living in so-called underground communities—safe houses or apartments rented with phony names and telephone listings, where people could hide out, knowing that their locations and basic information were not generally available.

Even though Sara Jane was now known in the radical community to have been a government informant, she managed to function at some level within the underground communities from January to June of 1975.

Sara Jane was adamant that she had quit being a "pig." She was passionate about her reform and told people she was no longer a tool of the FBI. She said she wanted to share what she knew about the government with her radical friends, but she was still lying to them, still using them for information that she carried back to the FBI.

Even Sara Jane was mystified by her success at doubling. "It was incredible," she said in her *Playboy* interview. "The faster word about me spread through the movement, the more new people came to ask me questions—and the more information I was able to tell about what the FBI knew about what they were doing. I never volunteered information. But if they asked, I would tell."

Just as she reported on each side to the other, Sara Jane held each side equally in contempt in some ways, not feeling particularly guilty about ratting out either group. "Bureau folks were assholes who labeled anyone caring about human rights and dignity as the dupes of foreign governments," she told me in a phone call. She said she knew that they were wrong.

She did not feel remorse about squealing on the radicals either. In her *Playboy* interview, she said, "Here I was, walking around, an admitted FBI informant, and if they were so goddamned stupid as to talk to me, they needed to be taught a lesson."

She was totally committed to each half of her dual role. "Once I realized that that was what I was actually doing, I became very serious about keeping up my association with the FBI, because I began to see that was really the only way I could serve the left," she told *Playboy*.

She explained to me that her service to the radicals took the form of "telling people who thought they were clandestine members of organizations that the FBI knew about them, things like that." She had to be careful not to let on that she knew too much, she said, otherwise it would have been obvious that she was still working for the FBI.

One thing that is important to all political organizations is the industry that helps to get the word out. In the seventies this meant flyers, newsletters, and posters, all of which had to be in hard copy for internal communication and to disseminate propaganda. In San Francisco there was one print shop that was well known to the movement: Errol Hendra's Camera Shop on Folsom Street.

Hendra's shop was a well-run vehicle for publishing and printing political messages and information critical to any movement. Various activists in the Bay Area in the late 1960s and early 70s could often be seen going in and out of the shop. It was about the only place the alternative press could get their photos processed or have a newsletter published, and most of the alternative newspapers were printed on Hendra's backroom printing press. Among those who hung out with Hendra was cartoonist Dan O'Neill, creator of the politically satirical comic strip "Odd Bodkins," which ran in the *San Francisco Chronicle* until 1975. O'Neill's strip reflected the strong antiwar and antiestablishment feelings of the era.

Sara Jane was a regular visitor at Errol Hendra's during that period. She would get into political discussions with O'Neill about socialism, and they would debate solutions to the plight of the downtrodden and oppressed in the country. Hendra, a worldly Australian with a dry wit, and the acerbic O'Neill both found Sara Jane very intense, and that intensity made her an excellent target for their humor. "Errol would love to fill her head with nonsense," O'Neill told me. "We would really get her going on these political topics, and she would take it all very seriously."

One afternoon in the late spring of 1975, Sara Jane got onto the subject of violence as a way to achieve change. "Hitler tried to kill everyone, proving that large-scale violence doesn't work,"

O'Neill pointed out to Sara Jane. He told me he lowered his voice, and said, straight-faced, "On the other hand, look at who is president now, and who is the vice president. If something happened to Ford, if somehow Rockefeller became president, all hell would break loose."

O'Neill said that she got very excited at that point, shouting, "Then you agree with me! You see what I've been saying all along!"

Sensing that he had really started something, O'Neill backpedaled. He said he then told her, "All I'm saying is that neither Ford nor Rocky was really elected, that's all."

Sara Jane amalgamated what she had learned in the study groups and took it a giant step further. She was beginning to believe that all it would take to start a revolution was to topple the leader, and change would follow, and Rockefeller, she had decided, would not be an acceptable leader to the majority of Americans.

With that conclusion, she gathered up her things and marched past Errol and his customer, said goodbye, and walked out the door. O'Neill did not believe that there would be a revolt if Rockefeller became president, but he was sure that was exactly what Sara Jane believed.

Rockefeller's arrival in the vice presidency, as the potential successor to Gerald Ford, had resulted from the 1965 ratification of the 25th Amendment to the United States Constitution. The amendment was devised after the 1963 assassination of President John F. Kennedy, to provide a process for filling a vice presidential vacancy should one occur during a term of office. Section 2 of the 25th Amendment provides that, when the vice presidency becomes vacant, "the President shall nominate a Vice President who shall take office upon confirmation by a majority vote of both Houses of Congress." In October 1973, Spiro Agnew, vice president under Nixon, resigned in disgrace after the U.S. Justice Department uncovered widespread evidence of Agnew's political corruption. President Richard Nixon nominated thirteen-term

Michigan congressman and House minority leader Gerald R. Ford to become the vice president, and Ford's confirmation was relatively swift.

Eight months later, Nixon's public career collapsed under the weight of the Watergate scandal, and he resigned the presidency. Ford succeeded Nixon as president, and he then nominated former New York State governor Nelson A. Rockefeller to be vice president. As Rockefeller was not in favor with the right wing of the Republican Party, the congressional debate over his nomination lasted several months, but he was nonetheless confirmed in December 1974. Neither man had been publicly elected to his high office, but there were no indications of public protest in the mainstream press. On the contrary, Ford was praised for his selection of Rockefeller, and when asked about his first hundred days in office, Ford identified the nomination of Rockefeller as his number-one accomplishment.

With a net worth of more than a billion dollars, Rockefeller was not considered even remotely representative of the people on the street. Sometimes he seemed completely out of touch with the average American. He once stated as "fact" that the average family income in the United States was $100,000; on another occasion, during discussions of New York State's retirement plan, he needed to ask his aides what "take-home salary" meant. However, he had successfully been elected to four terms as governor of the relatively liberal state of New York, and he was well regarded by many.

Rockefeller was an easy high-profile target for the militant left. One of a number of threats against his life specifically investigated by the FBI was a Red Brigade threat to bomb a dinner Rockefeller would be attending at the New York Waldorf-Astoria on February 13, 1975. However, as the winter months rolled into spring, the country got used to Rockefeller, and people began to accept his role and position. Most people just seemed relieved that Nixon was gone.

Undeterred by Hendra and O'Neill's teasing—or perhaps unaware that it was teasing—Sara Jane averaged two visits a week to
the shop. On one occasion, in late May 1975, Sara Jane was being
coy about an item she carried tucked under her arm, which looked
like a small phone directory. In fact, it was a confidential book issued by the FBI to all informants. It was full of pictures of people
from the radical community, mug shots of everyone the FBI had
listed as a political dissident.

Sara Jane proudly produced the book and leafed through the
pages to show Hendra that she was really wired in, hoping that he
would be impressed that she had this inside information, that he
would see her in a new and different way. She wanted to be respected in the movement, to look as though she was serving the
community, and she felt that having this book might help improve
her status. O'Neill told me that Sara Jane told Hendra he could
warn his friends that they were known to the FBI, and that they
were not as invisible as they thought they were. O'Neill said that
he and Hendra dutifully pretended to be impressed.

THIRTEEN

HUNTED

It was 3:00 A.M. on June 9, 1975, and Popeye Jackson and Sally Voye—a white teacher in his literacy program for ex-cons and an undercover narcotics agent—had just returned from a party in Berkeley given by some mutual friends in the UPU. Popeye drove to his apartment on Albion Street in the Mission, where they parked, killed the headlights, and moved toward each other.

The night was dark, except for scattered pools of light under the occasional street lamp, and it was quiet. No one seemed to be around. Popeye and Voye were not paying attention to anything happening outside of the car. If they had been watching, they would have seen a tall, slender, black youth walking toward them softly and slowly, from shadow to shadow. The young man reached their car, leaned in an open window, and emptied the magazine of his semiautomatic pistol into both of them.

Those who knew Popeye's habit of constantly monitoring his surroundings would have expected him to be aware of someone stalking him as soon as that person got within a two-block radius. However, this time, instead of being his usual hypervigilant self, he was totally focused on what was happening inside the car. He was found with his head resting on the back of his seat, his eyes closed. Sally Voye's head was buried in Popeye's lap. Popeye's body was riddled with bullets, while Sally had just a few shots in her, leading police to conclude that he was the target, and she was killed only because she was there with him. Popeye's girlfriend, Patty Singer, pregnant with his child, was upstairs in their apartment.

According to the next morning's *San Francisco Chronicle,* the only known witness to the event was a thirteen-year-old girl who was looking out of the window of her apartment. When she heard the shots, she looked toward the sound and saw a young black man straighten up and run away.[1]

The execution of Popeye Jackson caused widespread outrage throughout the Bay Area's radical community. Hysterical charges and countercharges filled the editorial pages in the alternative press, and the reverberations of the discussion were heard in the mainstream media as well. This was clearly not just a random gang slaying.

Singer, Jackson's live-in lover and coworker at the UPU, was distressed that Popeye had been accused of being a snitch. "The charges against Jackson are false," she said. "The pigs do whatever is advantageous for then. They wanted to keep Popeye out on parole so they could get information from him."[2]

For weeks, the *San Francisco Chronicle, San Francisco Examiner,* and the *Berkeley Barb* reported a flurry of stories about who might have killed Popeye. Charges attributed the killings to be the work of government agents, underground guerrillas, or other radicals who believed Popeye was a snitch.

The killing may have been carried out by the New World Liberation Front (NWLF), according to a letter that the *Berkeley Barb* ran about a rally held in support of the six SLA members killed in Los Angeles. The letter said that Popeye, a supporter of the SLA, had spoken at the rally and criticized the NWLF, which might have angered the NWLF.[3]

According to the *Barb*, "He criticized the tactic of bombing only empty buildings. Instead, he urged attacks against members of the ruling class and their enforcers. The NWLF should have kidnapped a guard, he said, and held him for the release of imprisoned guerrillas." The report went on to detail a communiqué that the NWLF sent to movement organizations, saying that Popeye was distant at a meeting with the NWLF. It said he was acting as if he had something to hide, and that the group therefore decided he was a snitch, which is why he was murdered.[4] Similar stories abounded, but the most popular suspect remained the police. Members of the UPU said there had not been any threats against Popeye except "the usual ones, you know, like, 'We'll get you yet,' and that was from the cops." As Sleepy, a UPU member, put it, "Popeye had a lot of enemies, one of whom is [*sic*] the police."[5]

Members of various movements pointed accusatory fingers, each calling the other informants for the "pigs"; the accusations led to counteraccusations that those making the claims were "unprincipled in their communiqués" about the killing.

Specifically, a UPU staff member said in a letter to the *Berkeley Barb* that Hearst had ordered *The Examiner* to increase its third world, prison, and American Indian news coverage in order to appease the demands of the SLA. The letter stated that Hearst's support of Popeye was motivated by self-interest, that of getting back his daughter.

The letter continued, saying, "If Popeye had been interested in snitching, he would have made all efforts to keep up his contacts with NWLF, rather than be cold and distant or allow for any misunderstanding. The NWLF communiqués have been unprincipled in that the confusion sewn by such unfounded accusation made ripe the timing for the murder of Popeye."[6]

After Popeye's death in June 1975, Sara Jane agreed to be interviewed by the *Berkeley Barb*. Her association with him was well known. She planned to admit that she had been a spy for the FBI but that she was no longer working in that capacity. She convinced herself that she could refurbish the story she had used before and reestablish relationships with the movement groups that had formerly welcomed her but then turned her away, such as the Vietnam Veterans Against the War/Winter Soldier.

In mid-June, just before the scheduled interview, Sara Jane went to FBI headquarters on Golden Gate Avenue in San Francisco to meet with her handler, Bert Worthington. She told me it was her first time in that building since she had become an FBI informant some fifteen months earlier.

She told me about the conversation she had with Worthington, about socialism. She told him the radicals he so hated were good people who were only trying to make better lives for everyone in the country, not just the privileged few. She challenged him to come up with an alternative to the tenets of socialism. Sara Jane said Worthington told her to go back to church. "He wanted me to live the square life," she said.

The conversation then turned to the *Berkeley Barb*. Worthington already knew of her plans to go public because, in preparation for the interview, a *Barb* reporter had attempted to verify information about Sara Jane with the FBI. Worthington told Sara Jane that the reporter had been warned: If the story appeared in the *Barb*, Sara Jane would be in danger.

Worthington asked FBI agent Charles Bates to talk to her. According to Sara Jane, Bates told her they could not stop her from giving the interview, but that the story would make her a target in the radical community. If she did the interview, he suggested, it would be prudent for her to leave town—for her own safety. She claimed that Bates also said that he would not allow the FBI to be embarrassed; if there was anything the FBI did not like in the story it would be edited out by his friends at the paper.

Bates, in fact, was furious for two reasons. First, he told Sara Jane, her exposé would present a negative image of the agency. Sec-

ond, of much greater concern to him, it would put at risk the people and the work that the FBI had been doing to infiltrate the
movement.

Sara Jane shrugged and left.

On June 20, the story, titled "FBI Role in Popeye Mystery" appeared on page three of the *Barb*. It read, in part: "Ms. Moore said
she was contacted by the FBI and agreed to spy on a man she re-
fuses to identify other than he was associated with a cadre of revolutionary groups. She denies she informed on Jackson or ever took
money from the FBI for her information."[7]

On the evening of the day that Sara Jane's interview appeared
in the free distribution bins in the Bay Area, Sara Jane began receiving anonymous hate calls. The phone rang incessantly through
the night and on through the following days and nights.

During that last week of June, Sara Jane bought a .44 caliber
Charter Arms revolver from Mark Fernwood, a gun dealer in
Danville. She told me she was comfortable with guns from her
training time in the WACs. According to her brother Skip, she also
gained experience using a gun at home, target shooting with her
brothers.

"I needed protection," she later explained to me. "It sort of became open season on Sara Jane Moore. I had already had an anonymous phone call saying I was next."

Sara Jane said in a letter to me that she had an image of herself
being shot on July 4, with the neighbors thinking it was just another
holiday firecracker going off. She was not going to wait around for
that shot to be fired. She packed a duffle bag with shorts and T-shirts
for Frederic and a couple of loose flowered cotton dresses for herself,
snuck into her car late at night, and drove to the East Bay, where she
sublet an empty apartment. She found some sleeping bags, a card
table, and a couple of chairs for her furnishings.

She enrolled Frederic in a summer school program, because
she wanted him to continue to have regular activity in his life.

Nothing else was regular, however. "He had to remember two names," she explained in her letter to me, and he had to "handle his friends so they didn't know where he lived, but didn't realize they didn't." She had been afraid that learning to live with duplicity and deception might hurt Frederic. However, she claimed that he had "loved" living in a vacant apartment, sleeping in sleeping bags on the floor, and sneaking out to go to school.

They stayed out of sight for much of July. Then, hoping that things had cooled down a bit, she and Frederic returned to her apartment in the Mission over the weekend of July 25. The pile of mail waiting for her included a strongly worded "final notice" on a bill dating to January. She had had her floors sanded and polished by a company called B&K Services. She still owed them money, but had not worked for a month and was short on cash. On Monday morning, July 28, Sara Jane walked the five long blocks to B&K's offices at 4077 Seventeenth Street, to try to negotiate the bill. The conversation led to an agreement that she would work off the bill by doing some accounting for B&K.

On the way to the B&K shop, she realized that things had changed. She had gained weight, using food to comfort her in those moments of fear and depression; in three months she had gone from a size 8 to a size 12. Sara Jane felt fat, isolated, and totally abandoned. The members of groups that she had been working closely with for more than a year ostracized her. When she encountered a familiar face in the street, no one smiled at her or stopped to chat, and there were no calls about meetings or study groups. On a hot Saturday afternoon in August, she took Frederic to a theater in Berkeley to watch a movie that was being screened for the radical movement. Sara Jane told me in a letter that even though the theater was crowded, there were at least three empty seats on both sides and in front and back of her, and Frederic, who was nine years old, asked her why she would "want to be with these people when it makes you so sad."

Sara Jane was still considered dangerous to the FBI as well as to her activist colleagues in the Bay Area. She began a letter writing campaign to newspapers about civil rights and how the FBI was out to quash free speech, but she stopped taking Frederic to political events, saying that it hurt her to see him so upset. No one returned her calls or invitations for lunch, and when former colleagues answered the phone and found out that it was Sara Jane calling, they made an excuse about being busy, or simply told her not to call again, and then they hung up.

As the summer edged along, Sara Jane was looking inward, examining her experiences of the previous year and a half and trying to decide what came next. Her situation offered very few choices that made sense. Questions burned inside her about why there were so many real social inequities in America. Her search for answers, for solutions to those problems that fueled so much anger, was at the heart of her continuing activism.

In later years she wrote to me saying that, had the FBI not recruited her in May 1974, she would never have gone any farther inside the dissident forces in this country than the liberal edges. She told me that once she was inside the radical groups, she learned that the people were not the evil beings described by the FBI. She came to believe that it was the FBI agents who were wrong; it was they who were evil, it was they who hired dupes to "lay all kinds of shit" at the feet of others.

Sara Jane concluded that the FBI had used her badly. There was, however, yet another tile in her complex psychic mosaic. She had worked with the FBI and the SFPD, and she felt that she had been doing work that her handlers valued. Sara Jane had a hard time sorting out her conflicting loyalties. As she would later tell her *Playboy* interviewer: "'This is the part I don't understand about myself,' she said, clearly puzzled. 'People say, Why? And I say, I can't answer it. Once I realized that that [doubling] was what I was actually doing I became very serious about keeping up my association with the FBI, because I began to see that was really the only way I could serve the left. I realized I had been used by the FBI, whose tool I was,' she said."[8]

She knew that the FBI saw the radicals and civil rights activists as a threat to the established order. Worthington's words when he recruited her kept coming back to her: "You don't seem to realize that this is a war!"

She felt betrayed by the agency she thought she believed in. She shared with me a conversation she had with her control agent. "I listened with horror once to a bright young agent as he bragged about his abilities in the area of anonymous letter writing and other forms of character assassination, not of big important leaders, but of little people as soon as they showed any leadership potential. The Bureau's tactic was to cut down or burn them out before they realize their potential."

Drawing on the rhetoric of the Marxist study groups, she decided that she could help the "little people" rise up. She believed that India was an example of how democracy fails. She envisioned China as the shining socialist regime where the people had everything they needed and no one was oppressed. She did not see any contradictions between the early American ideals she championed, on the one hand, and China's repressive government on the other.

Despised by all, alone, with no protection and no one to stand up for her, she sought a community that would accept her. There was no mystery about the bent of the organization she had in mind. They believed in overthrowing the current government and replacing it with Maoist leaders. Their "violence now" revolutionary philosophy stated that in order to make change, you had to break a few eggs along the way.

In a letter to the *Berkeley Barb* on August 8, 1975, Earl Satcher, leader of Tribal Thumb, summed up their doctrine:

There is a frightening majority of so-called revolutionaries on this side of the wall whose rhetoric outstrips their ability to act in the most concrete and best interest of the political prisoner from the position that the political prisoner views the situation.

Nevertheless, the dangerous task of bringing down oppression in all its forms yet prevails and we intend to participate in destroying it. If we can ever get past the renegades, traitors, scabs who intellectualize and liberalize the methods of struggle while sitting on other peoples' [*sic*] freedom, the movement perhaps will achieve its historical mission.

Our regards to all the strong men, women and children fighting to attain the new world.[9]

Encouraged by the possibility of a new start, Sara Jane convinced herself that the best way to make a difference would be to align herself with Tribal Thumb. This group meant business. And so, during the summer of 1975, Sara Jane became increasingly involved with the group.[10]

Members lived mostly in the midpeninsula area south of San Francisco, and in Berkeley. One member of the group had property in Humboldt County, on the coast some hundred miles north of San Francisco, and the group had another house in Mendocino County. These locations sometimes served as retreat sites for the group.

It was reported to me, by an anonymous source, that a member of Tribal Thumb lived with Sara Jane during at least the latter part of that summer, and in the weeks before September 20, Sara Jane spent two days at the Mendocino Tribal Thumb retreat house.

FOURTEEN

TESTING SECURITY

On Saturday morning, September 20, 1975, the San Francisco *Chronicle* reported the details of President Gerald Ford's impending visit to the San Francisco Bay area:

> *Sunday, Sept. 21, Ford will dedicate a new law building at*
> *Stanford University at 4:00 PM.*
> *Monday he will speak at noon at a luncheon meeting of the*
> *World Affairs Council at the St. Francis Hotel.*[1]

The Stanford campus, in Palo Alto, is thirty-five miles south of San Francisco, a forty-five-minute drive down Highway 101.

Later that same morning, Sara Jane made a telephone call to San Francisco Police Inspector Jack O'Shea. She'd met O'Shea through the PIN program, where he was part of the local law enforcement team investigating the SLA. Sara Jane and O'Shea had come in contact with each other several times while she was informing for the SFPD.

Sara Jane told O'Shea she was tired of being hassled by the law enforcement system. She complained that law enforcement treated people who were politically on the left differently than those who were more conservative and politically on the right.[2]

She then told O'Shea that she was going to Stanford to "test the security," and to see if the system worked equally for the left as well as the right. O'Shea was puzzled by her reference to the "system," but when she mentioned Stanford he understood. That was where President Ford was to speak on the following day.[3]

"A red light went on in my head," O'Shea recalled in an interview with the *New York Times*.[4] He said he remembered that Sara Jane had a gun. He also knew that she was scheduled, that same weekend, to help the Treasury Department's Bureau of Alcohol, Tobacco and Firearms (ATF) "set up" Mark Fernwood, the leader of the John Birch Society chapter in Danville. The ATF wanted to check into the possibility that Fernwood was selling guns illegally. He was also the man who had sold a gun to Sara Jane three months earlier—the .44 Charter Arms revolver she'd bought after receiving death threats.

Recalling his conversation with Sara Jane, O'Shea quoted her as saying, "I'm going to ask you something that will make you recoil in horror. Can you have me arrested?"[5]

O'Shea's response to Sara Jane's question was carefully crafted. "If you carry a concealed weapon to Stanford, you will be arrested," he said.[6]

Alarmed, O'Shea said he called the FBI, the Secret Service, and the Firearms Unit of the Treasury Department immediately after his call with Sara Jane ended. He alerted each of those agencies, saying: "We may have another Squeaky Fromme on our hands."[7]

Only two weeks earlier, on September 5, Lynette "Squeaky" Fromme had waved a pistol in the air in Sacramento's Capital Park as President Ford was speaking. Fromme, a devotee of cult leader Charles Manson, had taken over the leadership of Manson's Family of followers after he had gone to prison for a series of gruesome home invasions in the Los Angeles area, generally referred to as the Tate-LaBianca murders.[8]

Based on O'Shea's calls, the Secret Service, Stanford police, and the Santa Clara County sheriff's office each broadcast an alert to be on the lookout for Sara Jane, saying that she might be armed and dangerous. Feeling that the president's life was at risk, O'Shea called the Secret Service again on Sunday morning, to see if the agents were going to pick up and hold Sara Jane. The Secret Service told O'Shea they thought it might be a good idea. To O'Shea's frustration, however, the Secret Service didn't visit Sara Jane's house to interrogate and possibly arrest her before she left her house in the morning.

O'Shea himself arranged to meet Sara Jane that Sunday morning, September 21, at an undisclosed location. He got her to show him the gun that she had in her purse; then she left for her morning's appointment. As soon as she left, O'Shea immediately called Mission District police and ordered the officers to seize her weapon.[9]

While the police were processing the warrant they needed, Sara Jane was accompanying an ATF covert team to Danville to participate in an action to catch Fernwood. The team included several U.S. Treasury Department agents, SFPD Detective James Molinari, and selected SFPD officers.

Sara Jane visited Fernwood's home gun shop accompanied by an ATF man whom she introduced only as Chuck. Chuck was posing as a prospective customer, but of course his main interest was to find out whether Fernwood, who was not a licensed gun dealer, was violating any gun laws. The police subsequently accepted Fernwood's claim that he was a dealer in antiques that included guns.

By the time Sara Jane arrived home, about 2:30 P.M., two San Francisco police officers, who had been dispatched on O'Shea's direction, were waiting for her.

"Do you have a gun?" one of them asked.

"Yes, in my purse," said Moore, unsurprised.[10]

Sara Jane had the .44 and eleven cartridges in her purse. The police found two additional boxes of ammunition in her car. They read her the formal Miranda statement of her rights and then took her to the Mission police station. Her gun was confiscated, and she was cited for possession of a concealed weapon, a misdemeanor.

While the police were reading Sara Jane her rights, an unidentified blond woman came out of the apartment and asked to accompany her. The woman, a member of Tribal Thumb, had become Sara Jane's roommate during that summer, and was seen by neighbors to be with Sara Jane almost constantly. As reported by a highly reliable *New York Times* source, Sara Jane had been closely involved with Tribal Thumb for more than two weeks before she was arrested by the SFPD. Furthermore, the same source indicated that Sara Jane had spent several days at the Tribal Thumb retreat in Mendocino and met with Earl Satcher's minions.[11] Satcher, it will be recalled, had talked openly about "destroying oppression in all forms," and he advocated overthrowing the government.

After processing Sarah Jane, SFPD Lieutenant Raymond White called the Secret Service from the Mission station to see if they wanted Sara Jane held for the entire afternoon. An unidentified Secret Service officer is said to have replied, "You don't need to hold her. We'll be in touch." The unidentified blonde sat quietly next to Sara Jane throughout the time at the stationhouse. Sara Jane was released at 4:00 P.M.—about the time Ford was to speak thirty-five miles away—and the two women went home.

As soon as she got back to her apartment, Sara Jane called O'Shea and told him, "You did that to keep me away from Stanford."[12]

At about 8:30 P.M. that same Sunday evening, Secret Service agents Gary Yauger and Martin Haskell Jr. came and picked Sara Jane up at her home. They took her to their offices in the Federal

Building on Golden Gate Avenue. While she was there, an agent telephoned O'Shea and gave Sara Jane the phone.

"I guess I'm in a fine kettle of fish," she told him. O'Shea advised her to "tell them what you told me and you'll be all right."[13]

The agent called O'Shea again and asked directly for more information on Moore. O'Shea repeated his earlier warning that she had had a gun and that she had been talking about going to Stanford University to test security for President Ford. He also shared the information he had. "I just told the Secret Service again what I knew about her," O'Shea said. He confirmed to the Secret Service that he had personally known her when she did informant work for the SFPD, and that he knew she also had informed for the FBI.

The agents interrogated Sara Jane, asking why she had been carrying an unlicensed, concealed weapon. She told them it was for her own protection; she explained the purchase by saying that, right after she had gone public about being an FBI informant in June, she had received death threats by phone and many hang-up calls. She also told Yauger and Haskell about her involvement with the Hearsts, and her attempt to help them find their daughter, Patricia. She recounted how FBI agent Bates and Randolph Hearst had each come to her for help. Following that conversation, the Secret Service agents told her she would be allowed to leave. When questioned about this decision later on, an agency spokesman would only say that the interview showed that she "was not of sufficient protection interest to warrant surveillance."[14]

For the second time that long day, Sara Jane was released from custody and she went home for the night.

FIFTEEN

THE UNLIKELY ASSASSIN

On Monday morning, September 22, 1975, at 9:15 A.M., Sara Jane made several phone calls.[1]

She tried first to call Agent Martin Haskell at the Secret Service, but he wasn't in. She called Bert Worthington at the FBI, but he wasn't in either. Then she called Jack O'Shea at the SFPD. The operator said she would take a message for O'Shea, but Sara Jane did not leave a message.

She made one more call, this time to Mark Fernwood, the gun dealer in Danville, saying she wanted to buy a gun for a friend who needed it for protection.

Fernwood said he was uncomfortable with selling her a gun for someone else. He told Sara Jane he would have to meet the woman.[2]

Sara Jane said her friend was not available but that she would come out herself. She arrived at Fernwood's home at 11:00 A.M.

"She was very pleasant and friendly," Fernwood said later. He said she bought a .38-caliber Smith and Wesson revolver and left.[3]

FBI agent Richard Vitamanti told me that Fernwood most likely had purchased the Smith and Wesson from a San Francisco police officer. The officer probably sold the .38 because the sight was faulty. Vitamanti said it was another agent who discovered this information, but he would not name the agent or the police officer who sold Fernwood the gun. The unnamed agent did say that it was not unusual for police to have—and to sell—personal weapons.[4]

Later, after learning that Sara Jane had gone directly from his gun room to San Francisco to shoot the president, Fernwood reflected that there had been nothing about Sara Jane's appearance or in her actions that would have aroused suspicians while at his house.

"Look at it another way," he said. "Here's a middle-aged woman, a divorcee with a child. She is dressed conservatively. There's no way of knowing she would do an insane thing like that."[5]

Sara Jane made several statements suggesting that she had wanted someone to prevent her from doing what she was doing. "I don't like to kill people," she said. She said she'd hoped someone would stop her before she reached the hotel where Ford was speaking. "I was speeding," she said. "I was hoping to be picked up before I got there."[6]

But nobody stopped her, so en route from Danville on Highway 680 to the San Francisco Bay Bridge she was loading bullets into the .38 in her lap.

After crossing the Bay Bridge to San Francisco, Sara Jane made her way to the Union Square underground parking garage.

The St. Francis Hotel faces Powell Street at Union Square. The square, which is bounded by Geary, Powell, Post, and Stockton streets, is a popular park, surrounded by an upscale shopping area.

Television cameras were stationed in front of the hotel on Powell as demonstrators lined the street with signs "advocating radical and left wing causes." One placard said, "Release Patty Hearst, Arrest Gerald Ford."[7]

Uniformed police, stationed every three feet along the wall on both sides of the Powell Street entrance to the park, kept a close but relatively relaxed eye on the orderly demonstration, and on the television crew that was desultorily interviewing several of the protestors outside the St. Francis on Post Street.

Sara Jane knew, though, that Ford would leave through the side entrance on Post.

Carol Pogash, a reporter for *The San Francisco Examiner*, said she spotted Sara Jane in the crowd near the hotel. The two women had met when Sara Jane was volunteering and working with the press at PIN and Pogash was covering the organization for a story.

"What are you doing here?" she said Sara Jane.

Sara Jane replied with, "The Secret Service visited my house yesterday."[8]

Pogash said there was no follow-up, just that statement from Sara Jane.

While Sara Jane waited with the crowd, she grew impatient. "When I got into the crowd I began worrying about picking up my son," she said in an interview. "I was worried about the time element."[9]

At 3:28 P.M., a presidential aide walked out of the side door.

"Before the president came out, another man came out who looked like him. Some people began to clap." The fair-haired aide had come out first to make sure there was a clear path for the president.

"I pulled my gun halfway out of my purse, and then I realized it wasn't he," Sara Jane said.[10]

Ten minutes later Ford appeared. Sara Jane said she was shaking when she pulled the .38 out of her purse for a second time.

Ford stood forty feet away from Sara Jane Moore.

"I wanted to be able to brace my arm across somebody's shoulder to steady it, but a woman shoved me to the front and I was right against the ropes," Sara Jane said. "The security was so stupid. It was like an invitation."[11]

Ford enjoyed meeting people, saying hello to them, and being true to his belief in being a public president. "The people do not want their president locked away in a bunker somewhere. They want him visible where they can see him and know he is there," President Ford explained to me in an interview (see Appendix). He said he'd stood still for a moment when he came out, deciding whether to cross the street so that he could shake hands with the people lined up on the north side of the street.[12]

At that moment, Sara Jane raised the .38 to shoulder height in her right hand, bracing it with the left, cup-and-saucer style. Sara Jane said she could see Ford's lined forehead centered in her sight.

The popping sound of the shot reverberated between the buildings on Post Street. The bullet ricocheted off the wall just behind Ford, ripping a scar five feet eleven and a half inches above the ground and sending chips of concrete flying.

She raised the gun again to take her second shot and at that moment Oliver Sipple, an ex-marine who had been standing nearby in the crowd, knocked her arm down. She never got off another shot.

Ford instinctively dropped down when he heard the bullet ricochet off the building. Seconds later, Secret Service agents Ron Pontius and Jack Merchant shoved him to the sidewalk. One agent pulled open the rear door of the limousine and pushed Ford inside and to the floor. Agents Pontius and Merchant jumped in and were followed by the president's chief of staff, Donald Rumsfeld. All three shielded Ford's prone body as the car sped away.

Things were moving just as fast on the sidewalk. Sipple pushed Sara Jane's hand to the side, and San Francisco police officer Timothy Hettrich, who was six feet tall and weighed 200 pounds, grabbed the cylinder of her gun. I recently spoke to Hettrich in an interview, where he told me what happened next. With all of his strength he wrapped both of his hands around Sara Jane's and the gun, pushing it down toward the ground. Sara Jane refused to let go. Hettrich told me that he was worried that if he could not keep the weapon pointed away from himself, Sara Jane might shoot him or someone else.

"I kept telling her to give me the gun. Give me the God damned gun. But she would not let go," Hettrich said.

Hettrich's other fear was that with all the mayhem and people running around, a fight could break out. If people started jumping on Sara Jane or bumping into him, the gun might slip out of his hands and thus give Sara Jane the chance to pull the trigger a second time.

Hettrich told me that at this point he decided he had had enough of Sara Jane's resistance and was not going to spend any more time attempting to talk her into handing over the gun.

According to Hettrich: "I took her thumb and twisted [it] back and that got her to release the weapon real fast. I knew there were Secret Service agents all around and I just raised the gun over my head and yelled 'here it is.'"[13] Secret Service agent Dotson Reeves reached them at that point and pulled the gun from Hettrich's hand. Other police converged on her, held her down, and slapped handcuffs on her wrists. FBI agents flanked her on either side, linked their arms in hers, and half-escorted, half-carried her into the St. Francis Hotel.

Soon, all of America would be asking the question: How did a middle-aged suburban mom become the first woman in history to fire a shot at the president of the United States?

SIXTEEN

"I ACTED ALONE"

Sara Jane was immediately taken into the Borgia Room of the St. Francis Hotel. There, senior agents removed the cuffs.

She refused to answer any questions until she was assured of her son's safety. The Secret Service had Frederic picked up from school in an unmarked car and placed in protective custody.[1]

At 3:50 P.M., Assistant U.S. Attorney Lawrence Callaghan Mirandized Sara Jane.[2] He handed her the statement to sign and asked her to tell him everything she had done on that day, September 22.[3]

Police Officer William S. Taylor, who was guarding Sara Jane, said she gave a rambling account of her actions. She said she knew she had fired too high. Then she demonstrated how she'd fired the gun, drawing her right arm up, with the imaginary pistol in her hand, and steadying her right wrist with her left hand. After Sara Jane had related the details of her day, she said, out of context, "In another minute, if the president had not come, I would have had to leave to pick up my boy."[4]

Then, surprising Taylor further, Sara Jane said, "If I had had my .44 with me I would have caught him."[5]

When asked who else was involved with her in this attempt, Sara Jane answered, "No one. I acted alone."

At approximately 4:30 p.m, Sara Jane was tucked into the back-seat of a police car and taken to the San Francisco County jail. She was arraigned that evening, charged with attempting to kill the president of the United States by the use of a handgun.[6] She requested a public defender. James Hewitt, a round-faced attorney with impressive experience, was appointed as her counsel the next day. Hewitt had spent five years serving in the U.S. Attorney's office. Then, in 1965, the Ford Foundation funded a public defender project, and Hewitt was selected to start the first prototype Federal Public Defender Office in the country.

Hewitt told me that, from their very first meeting, he realized that Sara Jane was not going to cooperate. She would only minimally participate in the legal proceedings that took place around her. She wouldn't answer any of his questions about the twenty-four hours preceding the shooting, or about the previous three months. She completely refused to talk about her past. When he asked her about her motive, she would say only that it was "complicated."

On Tuesday, September 23, U.S. Magistrate Owen Woodruff conducted the arraignment hearing and set bail at $500,000. One official at that hearing postulated, "This looks completely like a mental case, and if that's what finally comes out, that should wrap it up." Sara Jane, however, fought against being labeled insane, incompetent, or a "madwoman."

Hewitt said he could not convince her to plead "not guilty due to diminished capacity." She fought Hewitt on the point; she did not want to appear crazy.

"I have never been fully satisfied that she had a good reason to do so, but I can only assume she would rather go down in history as a crusader, rather than a demented malcontent," Hewitt said.

Two days after her arrest, and against Hewitt's advice, Sara Jane arranged for a jailhouse visit by Ellen Hume, a reporter for the *Los Angeles Times*. The story ran the next day. Frank Bell Jr., Hewitt's chief deputy public defender, sat in on the meeting with Hume, hoping to learn something of value to help Sara Jane's case, but he left feeling disappointed. The closest Sara Jane came to providing a motive was when she said she had experienced the same rage and frustration that many people feel.[7]

While Sara Jane was moving through the process of being charged with attempted assassination, her son Frederic was in the custody of the San Francisco Juvenile Authority.

On October 30, alone in the world at age nine, Frederic sat, small and bewildered, in the San Francisco Youth Guidance Center awaiting a decision on his future. It had been a month since his mother had tried to kill the president of the United States. If Frederic was hoping someone would come for him that day, he was disappointed. Frederic never knew his biological father, John Aalberg. He remembered, but for several years had had no contact with, Willard Carmel, to whom Sara Jane had been married for five years. Neither Aalberg nor Carmel was in the court room. Only his mother, accompanied by the sheriff, was present at the hearing that would determine the care of her son.[8] He knew nothing of his other brothers, sister, or grandmother in West Virginia, nor did they know of him. He had no one but his mother, who was sitting in the same formal hearing room—and was about to go to prison for trying to kill the president. Sara Jane had requested special permission to be there.

Social workers were trying hard to find family or friends to take responsibility for him. If they could not, Frederic was destined to live his life either in foster care or in an institutional facility. Fortunately for Frederic, Charles and Gail Roberts, a middle-aged couple from San Francisco, took him into their home.

Sara Jane said she had known the couple for ten years, which suggests that Sara Jane had met them when she first arrived in San Francisco in 1966. She never told me how she knew them or why they would offer to accept the responsibility of raising her son. Frederic lived with them until he graduated from high school in 1984.

I had a brief conversation with Gail and Charles. In a gracious but firm manner, they indicated that they would not discuss anything regarding Frederic or his family. They said that they had worked hard over the years to protect his privacy and to give him as close to a normal family context as they could. He had been through enough. I respected their decision and did not investigate further.

Immediately following Frederic's custody hearing, the U.S. attorney's office and Sara Jane's public defender, James Hewitt, agreed that Sara Jane would undergo extensive psychiatric evaluation as part of the criminal investigation.

On September 25, 1975, U.S. District Magistrate Owen Woodruff ordered the scrutiny of a full psychological workup, to be conducted at the Federal Metropolitan Correctional Center in San Diego. Sara Jane would be there for sixty days. The evaluations were required to determine her sanity at the time she shot at President Ford and whether she was competent to stand trial—that is, whether she was competent to understand the charges against her and to assist in her own defense.

As Sara Jane was being prepared for her move to San Diego, the FBI conducted a detailed personal background check and criminal investigation to find out if Sara Jane Kahn Moore Anderson Manning Aalberg Carmel had any ties to subversive or enemy organizations.

The FBI case agent, Richard Vitamanti—Vito, to his friends[9]—began his investigation in her hometown of Charleston, West Virginia. Vito's last stop in the investigation took him to Post Street, outside of the St. Francis Hotel. Vito graciously shared some of his findings with me.

Vito made measurements to gauge exactly where Sara Jane stood and where the president had been standing, in order to determine how close Sara Jane's shot had come to him.[10] He determined that, had Sara Jane Moore been using her own .44, or if the sight on the .38 had not been faulty, she would have killed Ford.

"She would have had at least a head shot, maybe even better, because she had been practicing," the FBI team reported. Across a 40-foot distance, her "shot was off about six inches."[11]

SEVENTEEN

GUILTY

The defense appointed Dr. Gustave Weiland as their lead psychiatrist. Weiland, who had served as the director of professional training at Benjamin Rush Memorial Clinic in Hyattsville, Maryland, before going into private practice, would perform the assessment of Sara Jane's mental status.

The prosecution's lead was Dr. Jonas Rappaport, a respected forensic psychiatrist with a reputation for testifying frequently for the government, usually to make the case that the accused was sane and able to stand trial.

Both the prosecution and the defense had a cadre of additional specialists who evaluated Sara Jane. Throughout October and into November 1975, Sara Jane was visited by a parade of four psychotherapists and two psychologists. Additionally, they secured whatever records they could from her earlier stay at Walter Reed Army Hospital after her collapse on the White House lawn back in 1950.

Throughout the evaluation process, James Hewitt, Sara Jane's defense attorney, would get reports from the psychiatrists saying that, in her own charming way, Sara Jane was being less than cooperative.

"She was not totally uncooperative, but difficult," Hewitt told me in an interview. "We couldn't find out about her background to assist the psychiatrists, and, while she would talk to me, she wasn't particularly helpful." Sara Jane talked only about what she wanted to talk about, and she'd never say anything about her earlier life.

None of the psychiatrists who evaluated Sara Jane came to the same diagnosis; rather, each attributed her behavior to a different personality disorder. Depending upon whose report one reads, she had a hysterical personality disorder, a borderline personality disorder, and/or she was bipolar.

The assessments suggested that the combination of all of these symptoms can be reflected in someone who has a pattern of excessive emotionality and attention seeking, an excessive need for approval, experiences extreme episodes of mania and depression, and an unquenchable need for admiration, as well as a complete lack of empathy.

Regardless of their differing assessments of her personality structure, however, each of the six consulting mental health professionals reported that they found her to be sane and competent to stand trial.[1]

On November 17, following these extensive examinations, Sara Jane's mental competency hearing was held at the Federal District Court in San Francisco.[2] Judge Samuel Conti, respected by attorneys on both sides of the argument, presided over this and Sara Jane's subsequent proceedings. Conti ensured that Sara Jane received every proper consideration and was offered every legal right and opportunity; everyone involved in her case would have to observe the letter of the law in his court.

Representing the prosecution, Dr. Jack Eardley, the chief of psychiatry at the Springfield Medical Facility in Springfield, Missouri, said that Sara Jane had periods in her past where she had experienced some emotional turmoil, and that she had difficulty dealing with stress. Stress, however, is not insanity. Eardley found

Sara Jane competent to stand trial, and he said that she did not suffer from any mental illness.

Also for the prosecution, Dr. Gustave Weiland described Sara Jane as a blank slate. He said that she periodically would adopt a role and play it out for a while, changing characters from time to time until they were used up. The role she was playing on September 22, Weiland said, was "Sara Jane Moore, vanguard of a vast and implacable movement."

"You never know to what extent she doesn't have things straight," Weiland said at the hearing.

"The trouble with role playing," Weiland had said, "is that after you run through roles like pillar of the community, businesswoman, social activist, police informer, and so on, there are less desirable roles that lead to incidents like this."

At the hearing, Weiland testified that "Ms. Moore presents as pleasant, intelligent, and at some times witty and bantering. She is always neatly dressed in the limited County Prison wardrobe. She apparently goes to great efforts to present the best possible appearance. She particularly seems to find it important not to give any impression of being flustered or in any way under great tension."

Based on the direct testimony of Eardley and Weiland, and the written reports submitted by the other evaluators, Judge Conti found Sara Jane "competent to assist in her own defense and to stand trial on the charges."

Hewitt then asked for another thirty days to prepare the case. He said the extra time used for the extensive psychiatric evaluations made it difficult for him to prepare his case fully. Conti replied that the requirements of the recent speedy trial legislation mandated that she be tried within ninety days. Hewitt argued that the defendant would waive that right for an extra thirty days but Conti said no. Having logged his request, Hewitt then said he would be ready for the trial in December, and he even submitted some of the files that would be needed to move forward.

Sara Jane had entered a plea of not guilty. Her actions were undeniable—she had been seen by many, and was caught on film.

Hewitt's strategy for her defense was going to be that, even though Sara Jane was sane at the time she was standing trial, she was functioning at diminished capacity when she took her shot at Ford. This would have meant that she was reckless in her actions and did not mean to cause harm.

"Sara Jane was not really seriously mentally ill," Hewitt told me. "That was the finding of all the mental health professionals who examined her," he said.

"Dr. Weiland felt it was a close call, and would have been able to testify that her conduct could have been the result of her mental condition. It was by no means a slam-dunk. My greatest fear was that Sara Jane would insist on testifying, and that the jury would be impressed with her clarity and intelligence," Hewitt said.[3]

Sara Jane would not admit to being insane or to suffering from diminished capacity. Her message—to her attorney, to her priest (Father Bill), and to anyone else who would listen to her—was that she was not crazy and did not want to be seen as such.

On December 9, Hewitt filed a "notice of defense based on mental condition," stating that Sara Jane "intends to rely upon a defense of insanity and mental disease or defect inconsistent with the mental element required for the offense charged."[4]

Sara Jane immediately stiffened her back at that filing by Hewitt. She did not want to be portrayed as crazy and she would not accept a defense—the only defense she could use—that would diminish her attempt as anything less than sane. Sara Jane decided that she wanted to change her plea to guilty, and Conti held a hearing on the proposed change on December 12.

Hewitt was strongly against her changing her plea. He felt she had a chance to try winning the case using the diminished capacity argument. But Sara Jane was adamant.

Faced with Sara Jane's implacable stance, there was not much that Hewitt could do. "So long as she was competent, it was her decision, after being fully informed of the consequences.

"Realistically," Hewitt told me, "our chances for an acquittal on insanity grounds were very, very slim." He said there were other possibilities. "A hung jury, maybe. . . . Political assassinations always have compelling overtones. John Hinckley was unique in that his modus was bizarre, and his reasons were irrational. Some of these arguments might apply to Sara. Juries tend to take crazy people off the streets," Hewitt said.[5]

Conti responded to her request to change her plea to guilty by first stating that medical authorities assured him that Sara Jane was competent to enter a change of plea. He told her that being mentally competent to stand trial and mentally competent at the time one committed the act are two separate and distinct situations. "I am telling you this to let you understand the consequences of what you are doing this morning. The right that you have to a jury trial and by waiving the trial, what the consequences would be for you. Now, I am very willing to listen to your statements."[6]

Pin-neat in a blue cardigan sweater and tan slacks, her curly hair cut short, Sara Jane stood ramrod straight in front of the judge. Her hands trembled very slightly, but her voice was clear and strong.[7]

> "I am not now insane in either the legal or medical sense. Six distinguished doctors have so agreed. I do not believe I was insane in either the legal or the medical sense on Monday, September 22, 1975. The two very eminent and extremely well qualified psychiatrists who examined me regarding the events of the day talked to me regarding their opinions. They agreed I was under pressure and that my judgment was somewhat impaired. However, they did not feel that was to the extent I was unable to conform my conduct to the requirements of the law. In other words, I knew what I was doing, knew it was illegal, had control

of my actions and made a conscious and deliberate decision to act as I did."[8]

She paused a moment, then turned the page of her statement and kept reading.

"To those of you who share my dream of a new revolution in this land of ours, I say, fight on. To those dedicated to keeping from the people what is rightfully theirs, I warn you never to turn your backs on those—on us.

"For these, and for other reasons, I am disinclined to participate in what promises to be a circus though called a trial, nor do I want to put on someone else's shoulders the responsibility for deciding what is an already obvious, and to the Government, a necessary verdict."

She said again that she was entering a plea of guilty.

Conti spoke: "You may think that this is a circus. I don't think it's a circus. I know it's not a circus and I am going to do everything that I can to see that all your rights are protected. Even though you implore the Court to allow you to change your plea this morning, I am not going to allow you to do it."[9] He ordered Dr. Eardley to examine Sara Jane over the weekend to assess her mental competence to make the change of plea; Conti set the next hearing for September 15 to assess that competency.

Conti knew that Sara Jane was not cooperating fully with the psychiatrists and that she had not opened up to them about her past; her conduct made it impossible to determine if there were any trauma-related diagnoses. Similarly, her unwillingness to be frank with her attorney constrained his attempts to build the best defense, as he didn't know what parts of her background might have contributed to her action, or who else might be involved.

Sara Jane was determined to plead guilty. Hewitt said she jumped up in court before he could stop her and again stated that she was pleading guilty.

Conti then, for the third time, explained to Sara Jane that a guilty plea would mean she would be imprisoned for "any term of years or for life," as the presidential assassination statute reads. She said she understood.

However, Conti explained again that if she would plead not guilty, by turning to the charges of a lesser offense—for example, assault—a jury could find her not guilty of attempted assassination. They might find her guilty only of assault, since her shot had not even hit Ford, much less killed him. An assault charge carried a maximum sentence of ten years, or a fine of $10,000, or both.

Still, Sara Jane would not consider going to trial, even knowing that the possibility of an assault determination was on the table. She stayed resolute and told the court she was very happy with the services of Public Defender Hewitt, and that she had given him all the facts in the case.

Hewitt then told the court, for the record, he did not think Sara Jane should enter a guilty plea, that he felt it was not in her best interest to do so, and that he had consistently told her so.

On December 15, in a fairly brief hearing, Conti judged that Sara Jane was mentally competent to change her plea. With the change of her plea from "not guilty" to "guilty," Sara Jane no longer faced a trial; rather, a hearing was set for the following day to determine whether there was a factual basis to support a guilty plea.

The pretrial hearing took place December 16, 1975, in the U.S. Court for the Northern District, Ninth Circuit, before Judge Samuel Conti.

Lead FBI case agent Richard Vitamanti had been meeting with Conti each morning, at the judge's request, to be sure that he was fully briefed on each detail the FBI was finding. Conti wanted to be prepared for anything that might come up in court that day.

At each hearing, Sara Jane's long-time friend, Father Bill O'-Donnell, sat quietly by her side as she waited for her turn to speak. Although they had moved onto somewhat separate paths, when he heard that Sara Jane had been arrested for shooting at President Ford, O'Donnell drove to the courthouse in San Francisco and presented himself as her priest. When asked why, with his strong reputation as a nonviolent man, he would offer his services to a would-be assassin, he said simply, "She may need someone to talk to."[10] O'Donnell would continue to be there for Sara Jane—by her side in court, quietly, each day, through her hearings on the attempted assassination, and for thirty years afterward.

Conti attempted to find out more about Sara Jane's involvement, and the possible involvement of others, in her assassination plans. His experience would prove to be as frustrating as that of the attorneys and the psychiatrists. Her minimal and carefully phrased responses opened more questions than they answered[11]:

> **Conti:** Were you coerced by anyone to do this?
>
> **Sara Jane:** No, I was not.
>
> **Conti:** Also, were you acting alone? In other words, were you acting in concert with anyone else, or was this merely an idea of your own—your own idea?
>
> **Sara Jane:** As to that specific date and time?
>
> **Conti:** Well, as to this killing of the president of the United States, were you acting alone, was this solely your idea, or was it somebody else's idea?
>
> **Sara Jane:** I can speak only for that one day, Your Honor that was my specific—I was acting totally alone in that instance.
>
> **Conti:** I don't completely understand that statement. Was there anyone else that assisted you in doing this act?

Sara Jane: There was no one who assisted me in doing this act.

Conti: Is there anyone who encouraged you to do the act?

Sara Jane: As to this particular time and place, no sir.

Conti: Well, that seems a little ambiguous to me.

Sara Jane: I don't think it's ambiguous, Judge Conti. I can answer; you know for me, I've taken an oath to tell the truth.

Conti: I understand that. You know you're under oath. What I am trying to determine is whether you acted voluntarily in this matter, and you did so of your own free will; and if there's somebody else involved in this matter, then I want to know what their relationship to this is, and whether or not they played a part in affecting your free will.

Sara Jane: I was acting voluntarily and of my own free will; and, beyond that, I am not able to say.

Conti: You say if—somebody else could be involved with reference to this?

Sara Jane: To this act, no sir.

Conti: What do you mean by this particular act?

Sara Jane: Firing a shot at Gerald R. Ford on Monday, September 22, 1975, that's what I'm charged with.

Conti: Did you intend to shoot him prior to that time?

Sara Jane: Yes, sir.

Conti: And when was that?

Sara Jane: Oh, no, I mean I did not plan at a prior date to do this and then not do it. Is that what you're asking?

Conti: Yes, yes, yes.

Sara Jane: No, no.

Conti: But your intention to assassinate was formed prior to September 22?

Sara Jane: Yes, it was.

Conti: And was that an intention formed alone, or did someone else assist you in forming of that intention?

Sara Jane: As to committing that particular act, that intention was formed alone.

Conti: You say, "that particular act." You mean assassinating the President?

Sara Jane: At that time, yes, sir.

Conti: Well, September 22nd.

Sara Jane: Yes, sir.

Conti: How about on some other date?

Sara Jane: I'm not going to answer that, Judge Conti.

F. Steele Langford, the assistant U.S. attorney, said that had he been given the opportunity for the kind of evidentiary development that occurs during a trial, it was reasonable to assume that "members of Tribal Thumb would have been indicted in the assassination attempt against President Ford."[12]

A frustrated court could not penetrate Sara Jane's obfuscation of her intent, whether it was to assassinate the president alone or to do so with the help of an accomplice or accomplices. There was enough anecdotal evidence to suggest that Sara Jane was not acting alone, that others were involved. Investigatory interviews[13] were conducted with members of the radical community. While no one would positively identity anyone, the undercurrent, the suggestion, that others were involved was substantial. No one was willing to speak for the record, and without a trial, no subpoenas could be issued. There was no governmental follow-up, no effort to go beyond Sara Jane's testimony. It is possible that, lacking any useful information from Sara Jane, there was not enough information to conduct an in-depth investigation of the role of Tribal Thumb. It's also been suggested, however, that the government had a clearly guilty suspect, and that the sooner they closed the case, the sooner the public would focus on things other than the inability of the several agencies to keep a middle-aged woman from attempting to kill the president of the United States.

EIGHTEEN

MAKING A STATEMENT

As the defendant, Sara Jane was given an opportunity to present a statement at her sentencing hearing on January 16, 1976.

She had been sitting in her cell, using every spare minute to prepare her statement. It was her turn to make her position known. This is her statement, as recorded in court documents:

My attorney said I had the right to make a statement at this point.

Would I counsel anyone else to attempt such an assassination? No.

Do I think assassination a valid political tool? Yes. Used selectively and with the purpose clearly and publicly stated, it can be, and has been, very effective. Recently it has been more often and most effectively used against, rather than by, progressive forces.

Am I sorry I tried? Yes and no.

Yes, because it accomplished little except to throw away the rest of my life, although I realize there are those who think that's the one good thing resulting from this.

And no, I'm not sorry I tried, because at the time it seemed a correct expression of my anger and, if successful, the assassination combined with the public disclosures of this government's own activities in this area just might have triggered the kind of chaos that could have started the upheaval of change.

How in two years did I change from a relatively normal middle-aged suburbanite to a would-be assassin?

And, yes, I do think I was relatively normal. Many of the people around me were almost as dissatisfied as I with the "system" and were looking for answers. They worked in the same causes as I.

In the peace movement, which grew into massive and sometimes violent anti-war protests, in support for the struggles of the farm workers in the Salinas Valley—in help for the Black Panther Party then trying to bring good medical care to the people by establishing free medical clinics in East Oakland—in new awareness of the prison system and its horrors through people like Fay Stender who spoke so well to our groups and clubs about her clients.

The murder of Marcus Foster followed by the kidnapping of Patty Hearst brought me first as a volunteer to the PIN program and then to the attention of the FBI as I met and began to work again with those I had briefly met or heard about during those fashionable liberal do-gooder actions of a few years before.

But this time I was faced with the reality, the very raw truth, of those things only spoken about before. Instead of a polite and articulate David Hilliard and Johnny Seale [Bobby Seale's brother], or a brilliant and well-spoken Faye Stender, I met with the people they spoke of—the angry, no the enraged black and brown people we oppress and close out of our system.

And the FBI directed me to people and organizations seriously working for radical change, whose dreams I found I shared—whose dedication I envied and whose goal, socialism, seemed not only necessary but also possible.

My natural inclination was toward the theorists—mostly well-educated white people like myself who studied and wrote but eschewed violent action. But the original reason the FBI recruited me was the search for Patty Hearst and the SLA so I stayed very much interested in and active among the angry and dispossessed the theorists only talked about.

So, there was working on me this combination of theory, which made me understand a possible and powerful dream and exposure to those who found their only recourse in violence. There was no coordination, not even any communication between these groups. The whole left as a matter of fact seemed disorganized, strife-ridden and weak.

And I realized the reason for this was the FBI whose tool I was, who clearly and correctly saw the strength and power of the idea of socialism, realized it represented a very real change to our profit-motivated corporate state and who had declared a total, though secret, war against not only dedicated revolutionaries but also against the progressive forces, even those working for the most acceptable "American" changes, such as civil rights because they threatened the established order.

I listened with horror once to a bright young agent as he bragged about his abilities in the area of anonymous letter writing and other forms of character assassination. Not of big important leaders; but of little people as soon as they showed any leadership potential, the Bureau's tactic is to cut them down or burn them out before they realize their potential.

I remember Bert Worthington, my Bureau contact, saying, "You don't seem to realize that this is a war." He told me, two years ago, that he thought the next two or three years were probably the most crucial in our nation's history. His greatest fear at that time was that the left would rediscover the documents and ideas from the first and second American revolutions and use them to spark a new revolution. He said that those words are as powerful today as ever and that properly used (actually he said "cleverly") the people could be aroused to these ideas and would fight again to achieve them.

Why is Socialism so compelling an idea? Well, compared to China and India thirty years ago similarly oppressed, famine-ridden, the people illiterate, the leaders corrupt. Both threw off foreign yokes, China went the Socialist route, the other, India, went the western-style, Democratic route.

Today India is still corrupt; their people oppressed, poverty-stricken, famine-ridden, jobless and ill housed while China's 800 million are healthy, literate, working, well housed and fed and appear to be happy.

In a country approximately the size of the United States, but much less favored in resources they have accomplished in 30 years what we have not managed in 200. China has managed with no help from the Western World (and since 1960 no outside help at all) to surround the people with all the material, educational, and medical necessities of life. Prostitution and drug trafficking have also been eliminated. What the Chinese people see is a valid system that functions as their leaders say it should. A united people, they have solved the staggering problems of poverty, hunger, disease, and crime.

That explains my political beliefs. It does not explain why in the name of a dream whose essence is a deep love for people, and a belief in the essential beauty and worth of each individual, I would pick up a gun intending to kill another human being.

When I was getting ready to "go public" regarding my spying activities, a journalist attempting to verify some facts was told by the FBI that if the story appeared I would be in danger.

The FBI with the additional suggestion that I should leave town repeated this warning to me. Charles Bates (lead FBI agent in San Francisco) told me that of course they couldn't stop me from talking but that I was placing myself in danger if the story appeared. He stated that at any rate he was not going to allow the FBI to be embarrassed. If there was anything they didn't like in the story they would simply see that it was edited out, that they had done this before, that he had "friends" on that particular paper somewhat higher up than the reporter level.

After that, it sort of became open season on Sara Jane Moore. I had already had a phone call saying I was next. That was just after Popeye Jackson's murder. Now friends and foes alike vied with each other to warn me, each claiming to have heard from sources they refused to name that I was to die, "offed" or at the very least beaten.

But beyond a certain point pressure and threats are counter productive. When one is threatened to a point where one is convinced; that is, when I finally accepted the fact that I was not going to be able to get away, that I wasn't willing to pay the price, the realization I would probably be killed ceased to frighten me. It brought instead a sense of freedom. The fear of arrest similarly disappeared. It wasn't if but only when again the sense of freedom.

When there was no longer any chance of being accepted by those people doing what I felt was positive constructive work toward radical change, I finally understood and joined those who have only destruction and violence for a means of making change, and came to understand that violence can sometimes be constructive.

But back to here and now and the United States of America versus Sara Jane Moore. In your shoes, what would I do with such as me? Well, first, I'd trash, discredit, and make me seem a "kook." With the help of the ever-cooperative press, you've done a good job.

The court listened. When Sara Jane had finished speaking, Judge Conti made his own statement:

> The thing that concerns me listening to Miss Moore's statement . . . what really concerns me most about America is how calloused we have become to crime and to violence, and we have accepted it as an ingredient of our daily life. And we are tolerating it. And, we allow semantics to pervade our way of life by saying if we are angry at somebody, or we want to make a statement, what do we do? We shoot them! Or we bomb them!
>
> And I am convinced of one thing, Miss Moore: I have practiced law for 20 years before I assumed the bench, representing defendants, not as a prosecutor, representing defendants, and I know one thing, you would not be standing here before me today if we had in this country an effective capital punishment law.
>
> And I say that because I know there is a segment in our society today, this is a big game you are playing, you are playing a

big game, there is a big segment in our society today that does not care about their mothers, they don't care about their fathers, they don't care about their children, they don't even care about going to jail. In fact, in many events, they have a higher standard of life in jail than outside.

There's only one thing they care about, and that is their skin. If they think their neck is in jeopardy, then there is one law that comes into play at that particular moment and that is the law of self-preservation. And, if you thought at the moment that you were going to press that trigger and fire that shot that you would be subjected to capital punishment, you wouldn't be pulling this trigger.

And, there are many, many people in this country that would not be doing exactly the same thing.

Why is it that we went almost for two decades without kidnappings in this country? For one simple reason: if people do it, then they got the gallows, they got shot, or they got the gas chamber.

But today we allow you to have your semantics and play your game, as you are doing it today, and if we had capital punishment, you wouldn't be here today, and we would be saving a lot of people by having capital punishment, because there are many people that would not be pulling the trigger, that would not be putting that bomb down to kill or maim—and this is the thing that concerns me about your attitude.

You say that the other countries are better than this country. I think anyone that lives in this country should pray to God each night that we continue with the type of government we have in this country. We have got 200 years, and there is no other country in the world that has a better system of government than we have. And I will tell you this, if we let down the immigration laws in this country, and any other country would allow their people to migrate to this country, we would have so many people in this country the country would probably sink to the bottom of the ocean. That is how bad this country is.

We're tolerating such things you are doing, and you take it among yourselves to be the judge, jury, and the executioner.

I asked the Probation Officer to ask you whether you believe in capital punishment. He said, oh, no, you don't believe that the state has any right to capital punishment, but you believe in capital punishment, and you do it with semantics. I'm not shooting the President as an individual; I am shooting him as an office-holder, as the President of the United States, not as the individual Gerald Ford.

You are not shooting me as Judge Conti but as a judge you want to shoot me. That is of great consolation to our society to have people fix in their own minds who is right and who is wrong, and you yourself would be the judge and the executioner and everything else rolled into one.

I can see how you have arrived at this way, because you are a product of our times, a product of permissive society. But, unfortunately you are a product that we cannot afford, and by your own words here. You have no remorse for what you have done; in one breath you say "Am I sorry for what I did? Yes and no." That is no attitude to have about trying to kill a fellow human being, I don't care if he is the President of the United States or the fellow that is a little shoe man down the street—his life is important to him. If you have got something to say, whatever happened to "the pen is mightier than the sword?" Whatever happened to that?

Sara Jane interrupted to ask: "Why don't you ask the people in Washington the same thing?"

Conti continued.

If you want to so berate this country, all you are trying to do and people such as yourself, you are trying to build your own egos, and you are misguided, and you are blaming society for your own personal faults. And if you can convince everybody that society is to blame then no one is to blame.

The only reason the President was not killed was not through any fault of your own, it was a malfunctioning of that gun. Your aim was straight. The gun shot to the right a little bit. If it were a correct gun you would have killed the man. It is a terrible thing for one individual to kill another individual, and perhaps, as I say, the only consequence it was a faulty gun sight made the attempt on the President's life unsuccessful.

The enormity of the offense and the hopeful deterrent, whatever we have, the hopeful deterrent of the aspect of imprisonment would lead me to commit you to the maximum.

So it is the judgment of the Court that you be confined to the custody of the Attorney General for the maximum term prescribed by law, and that term is life imprisonment. I am also ordering that all evidence and all reports that were in evidence and were used in this trial will be sealed by the Court and will not be opened until further order of the court.

There was little reaction to Sara Jane's sentence. The press had already reported, in detail, her request for a guilty plea.

Father Bill was there to say goodbye, but there was no family in court to support her. No one came from West Virginia, Los Angeles, or San Francisco.

And on January 17, 1976, Sara Jane began serving her sentence at the Federal Correctional Institution at Terminal Island in San Pedro, California, twenty miles south of Los Angeles.

NINETEEN

THE PRISONER

South of Los Angeles, U.S. Route 1, also known as the Pacific Coast
Highway, runs down past seaside towns that include four of California's most beautiful beaches: Manhattan, Hermosa, Redondo,
and Torrance. Just south of Torrance, the Palos Verdes Peninsula—a spit of land studded with stands of eucalyptus, pepper,
pine, and coral trees on rolling low mountains—juts west, into the
ocean. Gleaming two-story homes are situated on landscaped hill-
side lots and tucked into canyon floors in the Palos Verdes Hills.
The town of San Pedro and Los Angeles Harbor sit just beyond, at
the southeastern corner of the peninsula. On an island just beyond
the harbor, across the graceful Vincent Thomas suspension bridge,
sits the Federal Correctional Institution at Terminal Island (TI),
an all-male prison that, in 1976, was also a temporary home for
sixty female inmates.

TI is known as the country club of federal institutions, sitting
at water's edge, with a wide expanse of green grass in front and a
volleyball court on one side. White-collar criminals made up the
bulk of the TI population in 1976, including such people as the
eighteen co-conspirators in the equity funding scandal of 1973 in

which false insurance policies were created and fake profits were used to inflate the price of the stock. It was in this setting that Sara Jane Moore began her prison life.

Shortly after her arrival at TI, Sara Jane jumped into the middle of two issues that had upset the women on her cell block. The first was that the male prisoners could see directly into the women's rooms, as the yard where male prisoners would go outside for exercise was adjacent to the women's housing.

The second issue was that the women had more restrictions on their movements in the compound than the men did. The men had access, more often, to more of the compound, including the library and the dayroom.

Sara Jane staged a protest on these issues, by holding a personal sit-in—she simply sat down on the ground and refused to move. Her sit-in earned her an eight-week lockup in isolation, or, as it's known on the inside, "the hole."

She felt, however, that the cause was just and the price worth it. She wrote to tell me that, as a result of her sit-in, the men's yard area was reconfigured so that it was not directly adjacent to the women's rooms, "so then they can no longer look directly into our rooms." The women also gained more freedom in the North Compound, which provided access to the library and dayroom equal to that allotted to the men.

These protests expressed three consistent and continuing themes that were woven through the battles Sara Jane chose to fight during her years in prison. One was the unfair treatment of particular groups of prisoners, which at varying times included women, Jews, and political prisoners. Another was what she saw as abuses of power, particularly by the guards. The third was the question of dignity: She would not suffer personal indignities that she believed were demeaning and insulting.

The price of her misbehavior was high. Every battle she undertook cost Sara Jane months in isolation. Almost her entire time at TI, which was just over two years, was spent "in the hole." It would take a half dozen years behind bars before Sara Jane finally began to comprehend that the balance of power was weighted on the institutional scale, rather than the prisoners', and only then did she become more compliant.

In her letters to me, she wrote that the warden at TI had labeled her an agitator and troublemaker, and that "they" were trying to get her transferred.

She did not see herself as an agitator, but as a political prisoner. She claimed she was incarcerated because she opposed the current U.S. government. She would continue to comment over the years that she and the other "politicals" were different from the regular prisoners. She would also reach a point where she railed about how other politicals were being released, and she was not. Despite her own self-labeling, radical papers and later Internet postings did not include her among the imprisoned politicals on their lists. She never acknowledged that she was imprisoned for attempted murder, and that her target had been the president of the United States.

Sara Jane saw herself as a leader among the women prisoners. She agitated strongly on their behalf, and the other women—and the warden—certainly felt her presence. In her arrogance, however, she decided unilaterally what the women needed. Then she acted without consulting with them about their priorities, or the tactics they would support, or the price they were willing to pay. As a result, she was recognized for her willingness to take a stand, sometimes appreciated for it, and at times even supported; but, just as she had made but few friends in the outside world, she never succeeded in gaining either peer acceptance or a strong cadre of loyal followers in prison.

While much of Sara Jane's basic tactical approach was confrontational, she did work constructively on several issues.

I was the chairperson of the California National Organization for Women's (NOW) Task Force for Women in Prison. One statewide Task Force project was to improve the law libraries at women's prisons, in that the numbers of books at women's prisons were substantially fewer than at men's prisons. Sara Jane's sit-in for better library access at TI fit right in with this initiative.

She was also instrumental in forming a Friday Night Women's Group in the TI prison, that met every two weeks to hear speakers on topics that included education, health, successful reentry into civil society, and self-expression through art. As the coordinator of those meetings, I entered the prison on alternate Friday nights.

With Sara Jane's help, that group became the core of the second U.S. chapter of NOW chartered in a prison setting.

Early in the spring of 1977, a different and potentially dangerous situation unfolded at TI. As the women were preparing for bed one night, they heard continuing moans and groans from the women's shower area. These were not the types of groans inmates quickly learn to ignore—the sounds of a fight or of sexual pleasure. Several of the women went to investigate.

On the tiled shower floor, they found one of the prisoners in the throes of giving birth. Sara Jane and several other inmates worked into the early morning hours to help the mother deliver her baby safely in the prison shower room.

The pregnant woman said that she had asked the guards to take her to the hospital several times that evening, because she felt that she was in labor. The guards decided that the woman was not "sufficiently advanced in labor" to warrant medical attention, according to the prison's eventual statement to the press.

This failure by the guards directly violated the state's penal code, which stated that children should not be born in prison. Further, both mother and child were put at risk because there was no medical supervision of the delivery.

Sara Jane telephoned several of her reporter friends, including me, the next morning, and told each of us of the prison's negligence. I felt obligated to respond. First, I called the warden, Lee

Jett, and asked for the prison's version of the situation. Jett had no comment.

Outraged at the obvious indifference to this pregnant woman, and drawing on affiliations I had developed in NOW and in various other prison-related activist groups, I gathered the support of a rainbow coalition of women's rights, prisoners' rights, and civil rights organizations, and called a press conference at the Los Angeles Press Club. My position was that in this case, fortunately, mother and baby were both fine, but had there been any complications in the delivery, the ending could have been tragically different. As a result of the press conference and news coverage, I received several calls from the local press looking for more of a story. But I was not an expert on prison systems and I was satisfied that we had made the situation public.

At the meeting of the Friday Night Women's Group the week after the press conference, the number of prisoners in attendance was more than double the usual. Sara Jane called and told me those attending the meeting were told not to say anything about the childbirth event. As an extra measure, there were two more guards in the room than usual. As I entered the room, nothing was said—but the women all stood up and applauded for five full minutes, then took their seats. Sara Jane, who had helped organize this silent demonstration of appreciation, was off to one side, smiling broadly.

After a year at TI, most of which she had spent locked up in solitary confinement, Sara Jane began to realize that, martyr or not, political prisoner or not, she really didn't want to spend the rest of her life in prison. In this case, however, it wasn't possible to do what she had done so many times before—just walk out the door, lock the past in behind her, and move on to something else.

Sitting unhappily in the hole for days on end allowed plenty of time for Judge Conti's observations to reverberate in her head: In a jury trial the jurors could have decided to find her guilty only of assault, since her shot had not hit Ford, and that such a finding carried a maximum sentence of ten years, or a fine of $10,000, or both. She began to formulate a strategy to find her way out of prison by revisiting and reversing her original decision to skip a trial and plead guilty. She needed to develop a rationale to make the case that she should be allowed to change her plea and stand trial, and she needed to find a lawyer who would take her case. She decided that the rationale would be a claim that she had pled guilty because James Hewitt had not represented her adequately.

Sara Jane asked me if I would help her find an attorney who would take her case. A friend who had a small but full law practice referred me to Peggy Garrity Edwards. She had just started her own practice, and was willing to jump into something controversial. She agreed to take on Sara Jane's appeal, pro bono.

Sara Jane prepared an affidavit for the court stating that she had been distrustful of her attorney, that she did not believe he was acting in her best interests, that she was afraid to go to court with him, and that she did not understand the meaning of being adjudicated guilty.[1]

Edwards submitted Sara Jane's petition to the United States District Court, Northern District of California, on April 15, 1977. She filed a motion to vacate the sentence and set aside the guilty plea. Edwards's 27-page argument provided legal background to support Sara Jane's claims that she did not understand the plea properly, and that she did not have effective counsel.[2]

Judge Conti received the petition on April 26; he scheduled the motion to vacate for May 19, and ordered that Attorney Edwards be allowed to confer with her client at TI during normal visiting hours, subject to compliance with the institution's normal policies and procedures that apply to all inmates.

On May 3, Edwards prepared a motion for an order against the Warden or Acting Warden of TI, because neither she nor Dr. Martha Kirkpatrick, the psychiatrist she had hired to do an assessment, had been allowed to see Sara Jane Moore, despite the Court's order of April 26.[3] Edwards had been denied access on April 29, and again on May 2. She'd met with the acting warden, Robert Anderson, and was told that "denial of access would continue unless and until my client, SARA JANE MOORE gives prison authorities 'her word,' in advance of access, that she 'subscribes to prison policies and regulations that apply to all inmates.'" Ms. Moore had, according to said prison authorities, refused to give "her word." Edwards said that prison authorities could not cite any policy or regulation that was being violated by that refusal.

Edwards's motions were filed on May 6; I was unable to locate any documentation from the formal disposition, if any, of those motions, but, whether the message was formally or informally transmitted by Conti, Edwards immediately gained access to Sara Jane in the days following and two 90-minute time slots were granted to Dr. Kirpatrick for her assessment.

The hearing was before Judge Conti on May 19, 1977. An assessment by Dr. Kirkpatrick, submitted on May 16, was admitted. Kirkpatrick's statement addressed Sara Jane's state of mind at the time of the original hearing, concluding that Sara Jane had been under great stress and fear, and that she was acting under duress when she made her decision to plead guilty. Kirkpatrick said that Sara Jane had not used good judgment because she believed her attorney wanted to use an insanity defense, which would make it appear to the public that Sara Jane was a madwoman, and Sara Jane would not let that happen.[4]

In her testimony, Edwards addressed both Sara Jane's state of mind and that the time to trial had been rushed. Defense counsel Hewitt was on record as requesting additional time to prepare. She acknowledged that the trial court in 1975 had been mandated to work within the ninety-day time frame required by the recently passed Speedy Trial Act. But, Edwards argued, the legislation had just gone into effect and had not yet been interpreted and clarified through case law at that time. Therefore, it was at least reasonable to posit that the court could have requested a waiver for the defendant—but did not. Edwards pointed out that when the appellate court did get such cases before it, in the time between Sara Jane's 1975 hearings and the filing of this motion in 1977, their ruling was that time taken for psychiatric evaluations could be excluded from the ninety-day period.

"At the very least the defendant, it would appear from the record, was willing to waive the speedy trial and . . . that is a personal right that can be waived. The spirit of that act was simply to avoid huge delays.[5]

Edwards argued that Hewitt did not provide Sara Jane with enough understanding of the law to make an informed and conscious choice.

"Sara Jane Moore arrived at her decision to change her plea of not guilty to a plea of guilty as a result of a lack of information rather than as a result of the possession of information. She arrived at her decision not only without the assistance of counsel but in contravention of his recommendation. She entered a plea of guilty out of her fear of being forced to trial with counsel who was unprepared. In short, said plea of guilty was in no way the product of a knowing and voluntary decision-making process and clearly does not meet that legal standard."[6]

U.S. Attorney James Browning briefly refuted the arguments presented, including pointing out that Edwards's "argument comes very close to suggesting to the court that the defendant who wishes to enter a plea and who is competent to enter a plea of guilty, should not be allowed to do so under the law if the counsel objects."

Judge Conti then responded. He said that, as the presiding judge at the hearings in 1975, he knew "that after all the publicity had settled down and Ms. Moore was in a federal institution, that about fifteen months later, she'd be tired of sitting down there and she'd want to do something to get out. . . . You can't sit as a judge and not know that such motions do exist and they do come. So . . . you want to be sure that what the defendant is doing is proper and correct and right and that you're not going to be confronted fifteen months hence with a motion and psychiatrists then coming in and trying to say today what someone's state of mind was fifteen or seventeen months ago."

Conti reviewed all of the steps that had been taken to assure Sara Jane's competence to change her plea and her understanding of that plea. Following that review, he skewered Dr. Kirkpatrick's statement about Sara Jane's state of mind seventeen months earlier. Conti said that, on the basis of her statement it would seem that Kirkpatrick hadn't reviewed the extensive previous psychiatric testimony, and that he "merely would peg this psychiatrist as a soldier of fortune who will fight for whoever pays for her sword."

Conti then focused on Sara Jane's previous statements about Attorney Hewitt, reading a section from a transcript of a tape in which Sara Jane had been asked by Dr. Eardley "whether or not she was satisfied with the services of her attorney and Ms. Moore had responded, 'Oh, love him. He's delightful . . . I'm supposed to hate him because he is the establishment's own attorney . . . No doubt in my mind that in his absolute heart of hearts, he is proceeding in what he genuinely feels are my best interests both in terms of client and as a human being.'"

As to her legal competence, Conti also quoted Sara Jane's discussion from that same transcript of legal issues, saying that he wanted to "indicate for the record that we have here a woman that is very cognizable and knowledgeable of the procedures of . . . the law, courtroom procedures and probably would have scored much higher than most students who finished first year courses in criminal law."

Conti then concluded by saying, "And so it's the judgment of the court that the defendant's motion is denied."

Barely pausing to take a breath, Sara Jane began her next step eight days later, on May 27, filing an appeal to the United States Court of Appeals; she also substituted herself as attorney in place of Peggy Garrity Edwards. The Court of Appeals handed down its decision on June 25, 1979, which affirmed the decision of the District Court in denying the request to set aside Sara Jane's guilty plea and to vacate the sentence.

She finally had to face the reality that she was going to be behind bars for a very long time—perhaps for the rest of her life.

TWENTY

SETTLING IN AND BECOMING QUEEN

In July 1977, Sara Jane found herself back in West Virginia. The federal prison system had built Davis Hall, a high-security women's facility set within the Alderson Women's Reformatory, and they were moving high-risk women from prisons all over the country to this new facility.

The prison sits at the outskirts of the town of Alderson, seventeen miles from Lewisburg, the next nearest town, and 145 miles from Sara Jane's hometown of Charleston. Surrounded by woods, and with railroad tracks and a river running behind it, the facility is isolated and remote.

Within the prison, a separate entrance was built for Davis Hall. It is a double-gated system known as a "sallyport," which requires entering via one locking gate, and being closed securely inside a fenced walkway before a second gate is released and opened. The windows at Davis Hall were made of several layers of unbreakable polycarbonate plastic. An eight-foot-high fence with razor wire on top surrounded the unit.

Prisoners were brought into the maximum-security cells of Davis Hall from federal prisons in Hawaii, New Jersey, California, and other states. Sara Jane was transferred from TI along with seven members of the American Nazi Party, several members of the SLA, and Squeaky Fromme.

Within each wing, there were three maximum-security units to a floor. Each was a cinder-block room with barred windows and heavy metal doors. Each floor had its own kitchen area and sitting room in order to minimize the movement and circulation of prisoners.

The isolation lock-up was a separate room made of cinder blocks, surrounded by metal bars on all sides. The door was secured by double metal interlocking bars, which locked with heavy bolts and metal flanges. In a letter to me at the time, Sara Jane said that the sign painted on top of the door that read CONTROL UNIT should have read ENTRY TO HELL. As she had at TI, she would spend much of her time at Alderson inside that isolation unit.

In the same letter, she lamented that she was sad because she was so far from friends or anyone familiar. "I wish I was closer to someone who knows me so I'd have regular visits," she wrote. Sara Jane's family—the family that included her mother, her siblings, and her own three children—lived but three and a half hours away.

Sara Jane's son Chris told me that, three days after Sara Jane was transferred to Alderson, her daughter, Janet, went to the prison to see her. Janet, the middle child, was 24 years old when she made this attempt to see her mother for the first time since being sent away at the age of three.

Chris said he thought Janet's decision was ill advised, but she went anyway. He said that Janet told him that, when she arrived at the prison asking to visit, Sara Jane told the prison authorities that she did not have a daughter.[1] Janet was turned away.

Janet was not the only member of the family who tried to see Sara Jane. Warden Neagle, who ran Alderson beginning in 1978, told me in a telephone interview that one of Sara Jane's brothers called and asked to come and visit her in the late seventies, but that she refused to see him as well.

To my knowledge, never once, during the entire five and half years Sara Jane served in Alderson, did she communicate with or reach out to her family.

Carson Markley was warden at Alderson during Sara Jane's first year there. He had begun his long service with 39 months as a correctional officer in the West Virginia state prisons, and then moved to the federal prison system. Markley is a gentle but strong, easygoing man, with a very specific and well-honed philosophy of corrections.

"First and foremost," he explained to me during a visit, "there needs to be an atmosphere of fairness. Prisoners need to know that behaving well will enable them to be treated with respect, and with some reasonable privileges; that behaving badly will mean loss of privileges and additional constraints on their degrees of freedom; and that each prisoner will be treated fairly, no favorites."

During his years at Alderson, Markley won local and national recognition for his effectiveness in maintaining a calm and effective correctional and even rehabilitative environment. He had his own ways of doing things, without feeling bound by all of the formal prison standards. For example, on an occasional hot summer day, if things had been going smoothly, he'd simply give the prisoners the afternoon off and serve ice cream. He even got unanticipated national press coverage when he permitted the inmates to set up a variety of booths for a Labor Day celebration fair, including a booth at which he sat in the dunking chair for a "hit the target and dunk the warden" ball toss.

One spring day in 1979, however, he wondered if his approach might have lost its effectiveness. One of the guards called to tell him that all the women were at their workstations, but that no one was doing any work. Work stoppages were considered a major disciplinary issue within the system. Markley got his chief of guards, and the two quickly walked out across the sun-drenched compound to the work area. As he walked into that sector, the women all turned around and looked hard at him for a minute. Then they all smiled, said "April Fools!" and laughingly went back to work.

Shortly after her arrival at Alderson, Sara Jane complained to Markley that she thought her mail was not being delivered to her. Markley read her note, left his office, and walked to the mailroom to check on her behalf. Then he walked over to her cell inside Davis Hall and let her know that he had looked into it personally.

"First, I stopped by at the mailroom, asked them to be sure that there were no delays, and to particularly keep an eye on Sara Jane's mail for the next couple of weeks to assure smooth processing. Then, after a week, and again after three weeks, I stopped by to see Sara Jane and ask how her mail was. She said there did not seem to be problems any longer. That was the only time any concerns from Sara Jane reached my office."

Sara Jane was fanatical about staying connected to the outside world in whatever ways she could. She was a voracious reader of books and craved magazines—one or two friends would buy subscriptions for her from time to time. She earned a reputation as being the first in line at the bookmobile, a library on wheels that visited the prison every two weeks.

When the prison system moved her across the country to West Virginia, her NOW membership papers did not follow quickly enough to suit her. She became distraught. She was so upset that her transferred membership card had not arrived that she was willing to pay for a second membership, even though her funds were limited, in order to continue the affiliation.

"I must continue to exist other than as a number behind bars," she wrote to me, saying that one of the ways to accomplish that is "to remain a part of something beyond the walls."

It did not take long for Sara Jane's familiar behavioral patterns to emerge at Alderson. There would be a paragraph in almost every letter she wrote to me describing a period in lock-up or in solitary confinement. "After a little over three months in the Long Term Segregation Unit, strictly confined, I'm back on full lock-up status," one letter read. Being in lock-up, however, did give her lots of time to write. Her letters, which sometimes numbered eight pages, delivered a constant refrain of loneliness and seclusion.

The isolation cell, as she described it, was filthy. There was no outlet for her radio, so she did not know what was going on in the world; and the light switch was outside in the hall, so the light was on in her cell twenty-four hours a day. The isolation cells were about half the size of regular cells—five feet by eight feet. Davis Hall at Alderson was quite an unhappy change from the country club atmosphere of TI, and that proved even more so after Warden Markley departed.

Sara Jane said she maintained an active correspondence with many people, although she never discussed them with me. She wrote that she was going through a very bad time simply because she was so far from everyone and that she sorely missed California; she feared she was losing her friends.

In January 1979 Sara Jane wrote to me that she was reaching a breaking point because she felt she was losing her dignity in the prison system. The prison staff was continually singling her out for harsh treatment and punishment. "I was constantly treated different from other prisoners," she complained. And when she was allowed out of maximum security and placed again among the rest of the general population, the other prisoners used to verbally and physically harass her.

She became angry when a guard asked her for a routine urine sample. The Bureau of Prisons says it regularly and randomly checks prisoners for drug and alcohol use. Sara Jane's name came up on the random sample list that month. Sara Jane saw it differently. In a letter to me she wrote, "I had no history of drug use and I vehemently oppose it."

For Sara Jane, it was the latest in another long string of harassment techniques. She refused to cooperate, and was placed again in the hole for punishment, in high security detention, for more than a week.

"I knew when I went through those doors of Davis Hall they would never leave me alone," she wrote.

When Sara Jane finally got out of that stay in the hole and returned to the general population, she was at wit's end, and she planned an escape.

On February 5, 1979, Sara Jane and another inmate, Marlene Martino, who was serving a life sentence for conspiracy to commit murder, were missing at bed count. They had each climbed up, over, and down the other side of a twelve-foot fence that was topped with barbed wire and made their way through the woods. Sara Jane was shivering in a light dress; Martino was better dressed for the cold and damp prison surroundings. They walked in the frigid night air until eighteen-year-old David Ross, driving through the area from New York, saw the two women walking alone and picked them up. The women told Ross that their car had broken down and they needed to get to a pay phone.[2]

Ross drove the women to Lewisburg, seventeen miles from the prison. From there, the women took a taxi to the next town, White Sulphur Springs. It was midnight when they approached the

Greenbrier Hotel. A local police officer driving by on his rounds said he knew instantly that they were neither locals nor tourists out for a midnight stroll on a freezing night. He drove up next to them and asked their names. Sara Jane said her name was Virginia. The cop was wary enough not to try to collar them alone. He called a security guard from the resort hotel, and together they made the arrest.[3]

Sara Jane's and Marlene's flight from incarceration had lasted less than four hours.

For several days after the escape, the Secret Service called on each person on Sara Jane's correspondence list. I got such a visit, in California, three thousand miles from Alderson. A number of us who had connections to Sara Jane found out later that her description of these visits was accurate; they were meant to harass anyone who might be considered to be her friend, rather than to get information on her whereabouts.

Sara Jane did not write to me about her escape until she was going to trial for the offense in April 1979. She told me that before she flew the coop she had destroyed all the letters and photos in her prison cell, saying that that activity would protect her friends. It may also have been to make it harder for lawmen to know where to look for her.

At Martino's request, the women were tried separately. Martino claimed Sara Jane had held a knife to her throat and forced her to join the escape. She said Sara Jane laughed hysterically, like a mad woman, frightening Martino. Martino had escaped from Alderson once before, when out for a doctor's visit. Martino's defense said Sara Jane was going to use Martino's knowledge of the area to help in her own escape.[4]

Sara Jane's defense team denied these claims and said Martino was a willing participant. Martino, who had recently had a personal religious revival, had used the excuse that she wanted to go to the chapel to get out of her cell block that evening. Sara Jane's defense team pointed out that Martino was wearing four layers of clothing under her coat, clearly her own preparation for an escape attempt.

During the escape, Sara Jane had hit a guard with a prison-made weapon and was charged with assault. Reports on the degree of injury varied. Warden Neagle told me that Sara Jane had nearly killed the guard; Sara Jane referred to the guard as having minor injuries. Martino was injured during the escape, and Sara Jane was blamed for that injury as well.[5]

Sara Jane's attorney argued that it would be difficult to force someone to climb over a twelve-foot fence against her will.

Martino's lawyer rebutted that, if your life were threatened, you would find a way to get over the fence.

As for Martino's injuries, Sara Jane's lawyer pointed out that a person could easily injure herself climbing over a twelve-foot fence topped with barbed wire, and that it would be impossible to prove that Sara Jane had caused those injuries.[6]

In her letters, Sara Jane continued to paint reality as she wanted it to be. She was adamant that she did not kidnap Martino or injure her in any way. She said Martino was just trying to get out of the escape rap and was using Sara Jane to do it.

Sara Jane wrote, "Did I kidnap the woman? NO! Did I inflict her injury? NO! Was her injury my fault? Yes and No."

Sara Jane went on about her escape in the letter, asking and answering questions herself. "Were the implements intended to be weapons? Yes and no. Were they used as weapons? NO! Can I defend myself from her charge? No!"

A CBS television correspondent interviewed Sara Jane shortly after the two women were captured. Sara Jane said, "It was my intent that, when I had used the knowledge that she [Martino] had, to abandon her, if that were feasible, and to kill her, if it was not . . ."[7]

In the end, Sara Jane was found guilty of escape; the sentence added two years to her life sentence, to be served consecutively, and a $5,000 fine. Marlene Martino was also found guilty of escape in a separate trial but was given a harsher sentence of $10,000 and five years in prison.

TWENTY-ONE

SOLITARY

Sara Jane got out of solitary confinement in April 1979 and went right back in again in May for another thirty-day stint; she had again refused to obey the guards' orders to supply a urine sample or submit to a search. She wrote to me saying that if they gave her the same directive when she got out of solitary, she would continue to refuse and she'd be kept in isolation.

Sara Jane described the guards to me as "sick, petty, frightened half-creatures . . . [with] distorted minds, mutilated consciences . . . their power are [*sic*] solely that of key and force." She said that they feared the prisoners because the prisoners were willing to think, feel, and dare to try to change things. She said she personally fought against the coercion of the guards, saying, however, that while she would not throw urine on the guards herself, she admired those prisoners who did.

Sara Jane was outwardly quiescent for several months during the summer of 1979 as she continued her time in isolation. In August, she mailed out a batch of press releases, including one in a letter to me, announcing that she had started a hunger strike. The release said that she had stopped eating; except for water and a daily vitamin pill, on August 10, 1979, and that she would fast to her death if necessary to get out of the special segregation unit. The release went on to say, "I am conscious of the permanent physical damage that resulted from previous hunger strikes. I am also conscious of deaths of other prisoners in similar situations. However, the outrage of illegal acts by prison administrators calls for drastic countermeasures."

Sara Jane's issue was that prisoners could be held in special detention—in isolation—for weeks and months at a time, for twenty-three hours a day, with no recourse and no end date. She said that ten women were being held in special detention at Alderson beyond what she called the "ninety-day limit" for inmates, determined by the Department of Justice. Jack Beverly, the acting warden at the time, said that there was no specific time limit for isolation and that special detention ended only when the staff felt confident that an inmate could be trusted. None of the other nine women, a group that included Marlene Martino and Squeaky Fromme, joined her hunger strike. Sara Jane was, once again, fighting against what she saw as the arbitrary use of power, fighting it alone, and seeking to draw the press in on her behalf.

On August 16, six days into her fast, she appeared to be doing remarkably well. Sara Jane called her friend Mary Neiswender, a reporter for the *Long Beach* (California) *Press-Telegram*, and asked Mary to issue another press release on her hunger strike. Mary complied. On that same day, two guards went into Sara Jane's cell to search for food items. They found and removed envelopes of hot chocolate, cups of dehydrated soup, tea, and Diet Pepsi.

On the twelfth day of her hunger strike, she sent a full-page, single-spaced typed letter addressed to her "friends and supporters," describing the events of the security unit, her health (she was feeling fine, not great, but fine), and requesting the names of additional newspapers in order to further spread the word.

Five weeks into her hunger strike, Sara Jane was still functioning amazingly well. However, because she was still not eating, she was placed in the prison hospital at that time; she wrote to me that she was still getting a full hour of outside exercise four times a week, "walking unaided" to the Davis Hall exercise yard from the hospital and "walking back and forth the length of the yard for about one half hour then sitting on the grass, talking to the women through windows." She said she would then walk back, on her own, to the hospital, "including climbing the steps to the second floor."

On the forty-second day of her hunger strike, she was taken to a hospital lockup. Two days later, she wrote that she was weak and slept a lot, but felt normal a good part of the day—and that she was thinking about writing a book. She said that she was only drinking water and taking a vitamin tablet.

In addition to writing press releases that confronted the issue of prisoners in special units, Sara Jane was engaged in a long-distance argument with Greg Dunning, a former neighbor back in the Mission District.

During her years in Danville and San Francisco, Sara Jane had purchased a number of paintings by unknown artists. When she was arrested, Dunning, who lived down the street from her, had agreed to take in and store her art for her. However, he could no longer do it. In a letter to Sara Jane, Dunning said that it was expensive and difficult to maintain the collection carefully and properly, and he could no longer afford those costs. He proposed to sell the collection and give the proceeds to her son Frederic.

Some six or so weeks into her hunger strike, Sara Jane had called an attorney to initiate a "grand theft" lawsuit against Dunning, because, she said, Dunning would not relinquish her art.

Dunning was furious at the accusation. He said that was the thanks he got for going into debt taking care of her art for five years. In a letter to her, he wrote that she valued her art more than she valued "the human life you tried to shoot away."

In September, Sara Jane called me in Pollock Pines, California, 150 miles east of San Francisco, up in the Sierra Nevada Mountains. She asked me if I would mind storing a few pieces of art for her, just until her son Frederic was old enough to take them. She said this art collection was all she had left. She added that if she were ever released, she would take it back.

I agreed. I drove my four-wheel-drive truck to Greg Dunning's apartment in San Francisco. Instead of a few pieces of art as Sara Jane had described the collection to me, there were almost fifty pieces, some rather large. Had I not been driving a truck, I would not have been able to haul them back up into the mountains.[1]

Sara Jane survived her three-month hunger strike physically intact. There was no permanent organ damage or memory impairment. By May 1981, she was her usual spunky self. When an Alderson guard told Sara Jane to do something she did not like, she told me: "My reply was explicit and inelegant." She found herself back in the hole.

Sara Jane badly wanted to get back to California. Based partly on her gradual and relatively increasing compliance, the Department of Justice transferred Sara Jane back to California in December 1981. She was billeted at the Federal Correctional Institution in Dublin, California, about forty miles northeast of San Francisco.

By June 1983, Sara Jane was once again in solitary. She wrote to me that she had had a chance to do some serious personal study and growth during that time, and that she had "come to terms" with resolving her lifelong struggle to incorporate the various parts of her heritage. She now claimed that she was Jewish.

Sara Jane had never before referred to this Jewish heritage. She had brought her son up in a Christian tradition, complete with

Christmas presents that she had asked friends (including me) to send to him on her behalf while she was in prison.

She wrote to me saying, "I don't know if I ever mentioned to you, but my father was Jewish." She went on to say that her father's family had been orthodox Jews who had immigrated to America at the end of the nineteenth century. She said that she had spent summers with those paternal grandparents, and that Jewish ritual had been part of those summers visiting her grandparents on their farm in New Jersey.

On her mother's side, Sara Jane wrote, there was oral family history that her mother's roots traced back to the Moroccan Jews who had been settled in Spain for centuries. When the family was chased out during the Inquisition and expulsion of Jews in the fifteenth century, she said, they left their Judaism behind, emigrating from Spain to Scotland, and then to England. She claimed that there were written documents that traced the arrival of the family in Rhode Island in the seventeenth century, and that also traced the migration of a branch of the family from Rhode Island to New Jersey.

Further, Sara Jane said, family records showed that Ruth's mother—who had been born in New Jersey—was a direct descendant of Roger Williams. "So on my mother's side I qualify for the DAR [Daughters of the American Revolution]," Sara Jane wrote in her letter to me, adding: "I wonder if they accept Jews?"

Sara Jane's sudden proclamation of her Jewish heritage was in direct conflict with her brother Skip's report of their family's background. According to Skip, their father, Olaf, was not Jewish. In further contradiction of Sara Jane's professed memories, none of the children had ever spent summers with their grandparents in New Jersey. Rather, Skip remembered only two short visits of several days each to the New Jersey grandparents over the years.

Skip told me that their mother, Ruth, was a strict Baptist who became more devout as the years went on. She took the kids to church every Sunday. Olaf did not attend often.

Later on, Sara Jane told me another story about her childhood home that related to supposed family ties to Judaism. Before and during her early elementary school years, strangers seemed to be living, for short periods, in her home. Her mother, the concert violinist, would explain that these people were visiting musicians who were playing with the Charleston orchestra. Sara Jane said in her letter that she remembered hearing that these strangers spoke "differently" when they talked to each other, and she gradually came to recognize that they were speaking different languages. Beyond that, however, the young Sara Jane had noticed there was also a lot of adult whispering going on.

It was only several years later, she said, that she learned that her parents had been providing a safe hiding place, a station on an "underground railway" for Jews who were escaping from persecution in Eastern Europe. The vehicle, she said, was the orchestra.

Sara Jane said that her parents had made it a point to provide gracious hosting for visiting musicians in their home, and that her parents would seek the inclusion of Jewish musicians who wanted to remain in the United States. Her parents then worked, she said, with an organization to help these musicians move underground to safety in other parts of our country, rather than returning to the persecution and the overhanging threats of death in their own countries.

If these events did happen, documentation would, of course, be scarce, and the likelihood of tracking down participants would be small. After all, those who stayed and those who aided them would have worked hard to cover their tracks—even though the passengers on the railway were escaping Nazi terrors, in this country they would still have been undocumented, illegal aliens.

Sara Jane's three brothers claim to know nothing of their parents' participation in a 1930s Jewish underground railway. They were, however, several years younger than Sara Jane, and they might not have been aware even if such a process had taken place.

To date, however, there is no evidence to support this story, including attempts to find any such history in archives in Jewish museums.

With her own version of her history as new inspiration, Sara Jane swiftly embarked on her Jewish journey in the Federal Correctional Institution at Dublin.

She told me in a letter that she had heard that Rabbi Ira Book, who served the small Jewish congregation at the prison, was quite an inspirational man, and she began attending the Friday night services he conducted. She said she was finding the services very interesting and enlightening, and that she "apparently picked up more" from her grandparents that she had realized. She said that she was not very religious and probably never would be, but that she was "fascinated to learn" about this aspect of her heritage, and "to flesh out the skeleton of bits and pieces picked up as a child." She had learned that Judaism is passed on through the mother. Therefore, since her mother was not Jewish but Baptist, and since she was not raised as a Jew, she knew that orthodox Jews would not consider her Jewish.

Beginning with her attendance at Friday night services, events unfolded rapidly over three months, during which time she became the cook in a newly established kosher kitchen.

Jewish prisoners had been struggling for more than a year to get a kosher food line established. To do so would require the assignment of space for, and the outfitting of, a separate kitchen to prepare kosher food. The federal Bureau of Prisons policy in effect since 1983 was that the prisons needed to provide vegetarian food to Jewish prisoners who followed the kosher diet rules, but nothing more was required.

The Dublin prison officials were not obligated to establish a kosher kitchen, even in the face of a number of court decisions ordering the Bureau of Prisons to provide observant Jews with meals that complied with their dietary laws. That was all the fuel Sara Jane needed to begin an all-out frontal assault on the Federal Correctional Institution at Dublin.

According to Sara Jane, that failing struggle had prompted several of the congregation members to ask her to start attending services. Some others felt Sara Jane saw an issue she could get in the middle of and that she pushed her way in, alienating and dividing the members of the congregation in the process.

A former inmate at Dublin told me that, "Most of the people in the group didn't want to be associated with her."

Whatever the origins of her involvement, Sara Jane felt that she had, once again, taken on the fight of a group whose rights were not being upheld.

With Sara Jane in their midst, the congregation filed a formal grievance under the Bureau of Prisons procedures. They also used the technique to bring pressure to bear with letters from the outside Jewish community that focused the glare of public scrutiny on the prison leadership.

The time that the rabbi normally allotted for weekly visits to the prison shifted from congregant services to meetings with the prison authorities to negotiate the issue of obtaining a kosher kitchen. Many of the inmates greatly resented that his time was being taken up with "Sara Jane's cause" and that he was not available for spiritual leadership.

Initially, three congregational representatives in addition to Rabbi Book would talk with the officials; Sara Jane was one of those three representatives. Even though she was one of the negotiators, Sara Jane had not requested kosher food for herself because, she noted, she was not considered a Jew by the orthodox congregation members. Nerves began to rub raw in those meetings, and tempers flared.

Sara Jane wrote to me saying the issue was that the other two inmates on the negotiating committee, concluding that they had more to lose if they got into a shouting match with prison staff, withdrew from the committee. Sara Jane, on the other hand, wrote, "I'm not afraid of these people, as there's very little they can do to me." She continued to stand defiant and fight, she wrote, because of her "hatred of the prison staff that was practically slobbering with glee at their apparent victory."

Sara Jane said she wanted to be recognized as Jewish by the prison and have her kosher kitchen and she said she would not quit.

She wrote and told me that when Associate Warden Marge Harding said to Rabbi Book, "Miss Moore isn't Jewish and as long as these other people . . ." Rabbi Book interrupted her, saying that Sara Jane had proved her Jewish lineage to his satisfaction, even though the lineage she had reported was patrilineal rather than matrilineal. He said that anyone willing to stand up under these circumstances and publicly declare their Jewishness was certainly a Jew, and that he, the Rabbi, accepted her as a Jew—hence performing a quasi conversion on the spot.

Sara Jane got her kosher kitchen, and the responsibility to be the cook along with it. She reallocated pots and pans from the regular kitchen without having either the authority or permission to do so, and she began to cook and serve kosher meals to orthodox Jews wishing to dine in accordance with their traditions.

I had moved from California to the East Coast in mid-1980, and Sara Jane and I continued to correspond. After my return to the San Francisco Bay Area in 1996, I was able to again visit with her from time to time at the Dublin prison. Throughout her twenty-five years at Dublin, Sara Jane continued to participate in the kosher kitchen. She drew upon the sewing skills learned at her mother's knee to teach herself cross-stitching; she then began to teach that skill to other inmates. She and her students each won prizes for the cross-stitching over time with entries they submitted to local competitions.

She learned basic computer skills, and, drawing on those skills and her accounting background, she was able to get assigned to an office job in the prison's financial department. In that setting, she taught herself SAP software (a complex integrated organizational management package). The federal prisons handle a good bit of the accounting for Prison Industries, and some for other bureaus of the government including the Justice Department. She commented to me, during a prison visit in 2001, that her office ran the salary checks for the justices of the Supreme Court.

Carson Markley, the sage West Virginia prison warden, had described to me during our visit how most prisoners gradually realize that they can't beat the system, and that they gradually become more compliant with it. Over time, Sara Jane did become somewhat less confrontational, and she even began to create some associations with the guards that sounded almost friendly in her letters. That didn't stop her from earning her way back into the hole on occasion, nor did it diminish her zest for suing the prison system, as she did in 2002, in order to prevent the prison from removing the keys that prisoners had been allowed to have for their own cells—a suit that she won.[2]

In 2006, when asked about her feelings when President Gerald Ford died at the age of 93, Sara Jane told Vic Lee, a reporter from

San Francisco's KGO television station, "I am very glad I did not succeed. I know now that I was wrong to try."[3]

After serving thirty-two years behind bars, on December 31, 2007, Sara Jane Moore was released from prison to five years of supervised parole. She was seventy-seven years old. She is the only person who actively attempted to assassinate a president, successful or otherwise, to be released from prison. As of this writing I have had no communication or information regarding either her location or her health since her release.

In October 2008, Sara Jane contacted my publisher asking to arrange for her art collection to be retrieved from storage and returned to her. She provided no contact information but said that a representative of hers would be in touch to schedule the pickup. As this book goes to press, neither Sara Jane nor her representative has initiated any further contact.

AFTERWORD

When I began my twenty-eight years of conversations with Sara Jane Moore, I had one question: How in the world had she decided to try, and then been able to come within six inches of, killing Gerald R. Ford, the thirty-eighth president of the United States?

After years of investigation, I—along with the SFPD, the FBI, the U.S. Secret Service, and six psychiatrists—still do not have the answers to those two questions.

I was fortunate enough to be able to interview former president Gerald R. Ford in 2003. Ford had been a member of the Warren Commission, which investigated the assassination of President John F. Kennedy, and was therefore able to provide valuable insight, based on his personal experience as well as the commission's research, into how future assassination attempts might be prevented. However, as he said, "There is no formula for predicting who is going to attempt to assassinate the president. Lee Harvey Oswald or Sara Jane Moore. There is no way to tell."[1] Later, he added, "There is little wisdom in the world to know who might be a potential assassin."

It was fortunate that the shot Sara Jane took on September 22, 1975, did not kill or seriously injure anyone. That she was able to take the shot at all, however, shone a spotlight on two continuing failures in our national security protocols: how profiles are constructed and how federal agencies communicate with each other.

Sara Jane's freedom to act raised a question about how the Secret Service goes about profiling people who might be potential serious threats to the president. The specifics of these profiles are, of course, highly guarded secrets. However, in 1975, a forty-five-year-old mother, former doctor's wife, and FBI informant did not in any way fit the constructs of a possible assassin. The mistake that the several government agencies, and the Secret Service in particular, made in not holding Sara Jane while Ford was in the San Francisco Bay Area can be traced, in part, to the limited and inadequate profiles they were using at the time.

Determined not to make the same kind of mistake again, a team of two Secret Service agents visited Sara Jane at Terminal Island a year after the shooting. They wanted to try to understand her, in particular her motives and the behavior patterns that led to her attempt. Every year thereafter, for more than twenty-five years, on or around the anniversary of the shooting, two dark-suited agents would visit Sara Jane to question her at length. Sara Jane, of course, never gave them much information; but they continued to hope that they could gather information by observing her and establishing patterns. I have been told, off the record, that the Secret Service profile of possible assassins has in fact changed and broadened significantly as a result of this long-term analysis of Sara Jane and her actions.

Another major factor that contributed to Sara Jane's opportunity to make her attempt was, and has continued to be, a larger problem for the country: the lack of communication between the multiple branches of our security agencies. The Secret Service, the FBI, the Treasury Department, and the SFPD all had information about Sara Jane that should have—and did in some cases—made them suspicious of her. Had they openly shared that information with each other, a clearer picture of the threat posed by Sara Jane might have emerged.

In my interview with President Ford, he confirmed that the lack of communication between law enforcement agencies such as the Secret Service and FBI in 1975 contributed to Sara Jane's ability to go unobserved.[2]

In 1977, when Sara Jane was just at the beginning of her prison sentence, Admiral Stansfield Turner was serving as the head of the Central Intelligence Agency for President Jimmy Carter. Turner investigated the problem of interagency communication, and his research uncovered repeated lapses in the system. Turner found, for example, that the National Security Agency had withheld important information about the Soviet navy from the CIA. Vice Admiral Bobby Ray Inman explained that he had done so on grounds that the information was "tactical" rather than "national" intelligence. "This, of course, was a bureaucratic ruse, and the loser was the United States," Turner wrote.[3]

Turner proposed the development of an overarching, coordinating superagency, to supervise the various national security agencies and to integrate the sharing of information among them. His proposal did not find favor with the various agency heads, and it was not accepted or implemented.

After the events of September 11, 2001, the U.S. House of Representatives undertook an examination of the reasons that our security agencies were not able to warn the people of the impending attacks. One of the clear issues that emerged from the review, yet again, was the continuing lack of information sharing among the FBI, the CIA, and other federal security agencies.[4]

Twenty-six years after his initial examination of the issue, Stansfield Turner still saw the same problems. In an interview with the *Christian Science Monitor*, he said, "One of the things the Bush Administration is not doing today that sorely needs to be done . . . is to reshape the intelligence process. We have fourteen separate intelligence agencies. Seven of them are housed in the

Defense Department . . . and nobody is in charge. . . . The administration is dodging this one because it would involve riding herd
on the Department of Defense."[5]

In our December 12, 2003, conversation, former president
Gerald Ford also noted that the failure of the agencies to share information in 1975 had obviously continued to the present day.
When asked what he saw as the barriers to those agencies working
together more effectively, Ford focused on the political issues involved: "They all want their own turf," he said. "They get their
own money, and they have their own power bases. It is too bad, but
it is not likely to change. It is possible that 9/11 will foster some
small change, but not a big one and not any time soon, I'm afraid.
No, I don't expect any of those organizations to give up what they
have without a fight."

There is some hope that the Department of Homeland Security will be able to finally bridge those interagency chasms; but it
will take time to see whether the necessary links can be forged between the various agencies adequately and successfully.

One final and pervasive question lingers: *Why* Sara Jane Moore?
How did this bright, intelligent, and artistically gifted woman—
who might have shared her many gifts, who could have had a loving family to whom she might have passed on her guidance and
love, and who might have contributed her skills for her community
and for her country—become an instrument of potential death?

Those who know her will say, almost to a person, that she had
become unable to manage her inner demons—much to the pain and
distress of her family. Exactly what those demons were, though, no
one could say for certain. She hadn't shared much of herself or her
thoughts with her parents or siblings, and she continued that pattern as an adult. Later on, in an interview by Andrew Hill pub-

lished in *Playboy* magazine in June 1976, she responded to a question about earlier events by saying, "I never talk about my past life at all. That's the choice I've made."[6]

Individuals who had only the carefully managed disinformation provided by the media to draw from saw Sara Jane Moore as a somewhat disheveled, round-cheeked country club mom who missed by a mile when she tried to kill the president. Many were surprised to learn that only a six-inch-in-forty-feet gun sight error had spared the president's life.

Psychiatrist Gustave Weiland said, after spending multiple hours with Sara Jane, "We couldn't find out about her background to assist the psychiatrists, and, while she would talk to me, she wasn't particularly helpful."[7] He said Sara Jane would talk only about what she wanted to talk about, and never, ever anything about her background.

Sara Jane turned her back on her parents, her siblings, and four of her children. She lied to anyone whom she might have become close to and repeatedly misrepresented herself and withheld information, as when she told John Aalberg that they had so much in common because neither of them had any family. She told friends (including me, in a conversation during a visit) that she liked keeping her friends separated from each other, and yet that it would be so interesting if someday they could all connect and come together. It is therefore impossible for anyone else to know why she chose to abandon her past so often and so thoroughly.

Without seeking labels, Sara Jane's dysfunctionality was evident; but how much of her behavior was a response to the actions of the FBI? And how much did the COINTELPRO approach factor into her choices and decisions?

Is the FBI responsible for the mental stability, personality disorders, or sanity of its informants? Should the FBI agents have recognized this woman as being unstable, and therefore not engaged her in their massive counterintelligence dragnet on the radical organizations of the 1970s? It would appear that they did not do an assessment of her as a potential informant, and they did not give her the standard eight- or nine-month training for informants. Rather, they just threw her into the pond, to swim or struggle as she might.

One could make the argument that, had the agents not put her into the middle of the radical left, she might never have gotten the large doses of radical philosophy that gave her a skewed perspective on our government and society. Similarly, had the agents taken the time to give Sara Jane their usual "inoculations" training, she might not have bought into that radical philosophy as fully as she did.

Even so, it is impossible to cast Sara Jane Moore as a victim; she had the free will to quietly stop informing for the FBI when her loyalties changed. Many others did so.

Dr. Weiland summed up Sara Jane's personality well when he described her as controlled and forced, but clearly aware of her actions. At several points in her life, those actions included choosing a different life and leaving her friends and family behind to wonder why she had gone without even saying goodbye.

APPENDIX

President Gerald Ford interviewed by Geri Spieler, December 12, 2003, by phone.

The interview focused on intelligence gathering and government agencies, profiling of potential assassins, and information sharing between law enforcement justice departments.

> **Author:** Is there any wisdom about assassinations and assassination attempts that you can share that you gleaned from your study on the Warren Commission and from your own more personal experiences? Possibly how to prevent them, ways to investigate, or create profiles?
>
> **Ford:** There is no formula for predicting who is going to attempt to assassinate the President. Lee Harvey Oswald, Sara Jane Moore. There is no way to tell.
>
> **Author:** In 1975, one factor contributing to Sara Jane being able to make her attempt was a lack of communication between the Secret Service, FBI, and Justice departments. I fear that is still the case, which is why we were surprised on September 11, 2001. What are the barriers to getting those agencies to work together more effectively?
>
> **Ford:** They all want their own turf. They get their own money, have their own power base. It has been that way and it is not likely to change. It's too bad, and it is not likely to ever be any different. It is possible that 9/11 will foster some small change, but not a big one.

Author: In 2005, Sara Jane Moore will have been in prison for 30 years. She will be 75 years old and she comes up for parole. How would you feel about that, Sir, and if you were in a room with her today, what would you say to her?

Ford: We have a parole board that will take care of whether she can return to society. We have a good system that can take care of release issues. As far as sitting in a room with her, I will never do that and I have nothing to say to her.

Author: You said after the attempts on your life, "The American people want a dialogue with their President and to shake hands, otherwise, something has gone wrong in our society." If you were in office today, would you do anything differently?

Ford: I still believe this today. I said it then and I still believe it. The people do not want their president locked away in a bunker somewhere. They want him visible where they can see him and know he is there. The person most worried about me after that incident was my dear wife. But after two ladies came after me I had to re-think my support for the Equal Rights Amendments.

Author: The Presidential Assassination Statute passed by Congress in 1963 says that someone who attempts to kill the president shall be punished by imprisonment for any term of years or for life. That means an unsuccessful assassin would be eligible for parole. Should the sentence be harsher? Should an attempt on the life of the president be considered the same as a successful attempt? Do you agree or disagree?

Ford: Yes, it should. An attempt on the president's life should be judged the same, successful or not. It is still an attempt to kill the president and the penalty should be equal, whether they succeed or not. Just because the president is left standing may be a matter of luck, but the malice is the same and the attempt was to kill.

NOTES

PROLOGUE

1. Ellen Hume, "Why Miss Moore Fired the Gun," *The Los Angeles Times*, September 25, 1975.
2. Geri Spieler, "Balance of Power: Women and the Prison System," *Los Angeles News Journal*, October 1975.

CHAPTER ONE—THE GIRL WHO DISAPPEARED

1. Skip Kahn, Sara Jane's brother, in interviews with Geri Spieler, 2008.
2. The United States Air Force Auxiliary—Civil Air Patrol, http://www.cap.gov.
3. The National Personnel Records Center in St. Louis, Missouri, destroyed by fire on July 12, 1973.
4. "Bewildered Girl, 18, Amnesia Case Here," *Washington Daily News*, Spring 1950.

CHAPTER TWO—THE UNHAPPY HOUSEWIFE

1. Arizona Vital Records: Birth Information.
2. "The Silent Generation Revisited," *Time*, June 29, 1970.
3. California Department of Public Health.
4. Charleston, West Virginia Vital Statistics, County Recorders Office.

CHAPTER THREE—THE DOCTOR'S WIFE

1. Personal interview with Jack Palladino, who investigated Sara Jane while she was working for PIN.

2. UC Libraries, California Digital Library, *The Berkeley Free Speech Controversy (Preliminary Report)*, http://www.calisphere.universityof-california.edu/.

3. Mario Savio, UC Berkeley, December 3, 1964, at the rally for a Free Speech location on campus. Alexander Bloom and Wini Brienes, *Takin' It to the Streets: A Sixties Reader* (New York: Oxford University Press, 2002), 85.

4. California Death Records.

5. Academy of Motion Pictures Arts and Sciences, http://www.oscars .org/aboutacademyawards/awards/55_aalberg.html.

6. Personal letter to me from Sara Jane Moore, September 30, 1980.

7. County of San Francisco Vital Records.

8. Contra Costa County Superior Court Recorders Office.

9. Ibid.

CHAPTER FOUR—CHANGING TIMES

1. Radical America 1967–1999, the SDS-connected Radical Education Project, formed in 1966, Brown University Library, Center for Digital Initiatives, Providence, RI. http://dl.lib.brown.edu/radical-america/index.html.

2. Paul Buhle, *History and the New Left Madison, Wisconsin, 1950–1970* (Philadelphia: Temple University Press, 1990).

3. Frederick G. Dutton, *Changing Sources of Power: American Politics in the 1970s* (New York: McGraw-Hill, 1971).

4. James Kirkpatrick Davis, *Assault on the Left* (New York: Praeger Publishing, 1977).

5. Sam Green, director-producer-editor, *Independent Lens*, Film Series, Public Broadcasting System, 1969–1974 Series, *The Weather Underground.* http://www.pbs.org/independentlens/weatherunderground/movement.html.

6. She later claimed to have had an early and continuing role in feminist activism. In fact, she had demonstrated a strong independent and perhaps feminist streak in the late 1940s when she joined the Women's Army Corps, and she would later play a significant role in the chartering of a prison chapter of the National Organization for Women (NOW).

CHAPTER FIVE—SAN FRANCISCO'S RADICAL UNDERGROUND

1. Vin McClellan and Paul Avery, *The Voices of Guns: The Definitive and Dramatic Story of the Twenty-two-month Career of the Symbionese Liberation Army* (New York: Putnam, 1977), 56.
2. Ibid., 13.
3. The Venceremos Organization, a radical spin-off from the Venceremos Brigade, was the creation of H. Bruce Franklin, an assistant professor at Stanford University. Franklin was a former military intelligence officer and a loudmouth ultraradical Maoist.
4. McLellan and Avery, *Voices of Guns*, 72.
5. Ibid., 19.
6. Ibid., 57.
7. Ibid., 137.
8. McLellan and Avery, *Voices of Guns*, 20.
9. Based on a *Time* magazine article, "The Making of a Misfit," (October 6, 1975), 28; and James Brook, Chris Carlsson, and Nancy Joyce Peters, *Reclaiming San Francisco: History, Politics, Culture* (San Francisco: City Lights Books, 1998), 328. This information was also confirmed in conversation with Attorney Marie Ferreboeuf.
10. George Jackson, *Soledad Brother* (New York: Coward-McCann, 1970); George Jackson, *Blood in My Eye* (New York: Random House), 1972.
11. Irving Howe and Michael Harrington, *The Seventies: Problems and Proposals* (New York: Harper & Row, 1972), 238.
12. Earl Sands and Bennett Cohen, *Zebra Murders: A Season of Killing, Racial Madness, and Civil Rights* (New York: Arcade Publishing, 1997), 129.
13. Ibid., 104.
14. Ibid., 225.
15. Philip A. Klinker and Rogers M. Smith, *The Unsteady March: The Rise and Decline of Racial Equality in America* (Chicago: University of Chicago Press, 1999), 288.
16. Frederick G. Dutton, *Changing Sources of Power American Politics in the 1970s* (New York: McGraw-Hill, 1971), 248. Frederick Dutton was on the Cabinet for President John Kennedy, Assistant U.S. Secretary of State for Congressional Relations for Robert F. Kennedy.
17. *Changing Sources of Power*, 225.

18.   *The Unsteady March,* 307.

CHAPTER SIX-THE WOULD-BE ACTIVIST

1.   Vin McLellan and Paul Avery, *The Voices of Guns: The Definitive and Dramatic Story of the Twenty-two-month Career of the Symbionese Liberation Army* (New York: Putnam, 1977), 20.
2.   Ibid., 13.

CHAPTER SEVEN-THE ACCOUNTANT

1.   "Hearst Says He'll Offer A Food Plan in 48 Hours," *San Francisco Chronicle,* February 14, 1974.

CHAPTER EIGHT-FEDERAL STRANGLEHOLD

1.   Intelligence Activities and The Rights of Americans, Final Report of the Select Committee to Governmental with Respect to Intelligence Activities (Church Committee Report), United States Senate Together with Additional, Supplemental and Separate Views, Book One, April 26 (legislative day, April 14), 1976.
2.   A memo from J. Edgar Hoover to the FBI Field Offices initiated COINTELPRO action against the New Left, as quoted in Tom Hayden, *Reunion: A Memoir* (New York: Random House, 1988), 42.
3.   Intelligence Activities and The Rights of Americans, Book One.
4.   Ibid.
5.   Ibid.
6.   Ibid.
7.   Carl Stern, professor of communications, George Washington University, in interview with Geri Spieler, March, 2008.
8.   Morton Halperin, Jerry Berman, Robert Borosage, and Christine Marwick, *The Lawless State: The Crimes of the U.S. Intelligence Agencies* (New York: Penguin Books, 1976), 77.
9.   Ibid.
10.   Ronald Kessler, *The Bureau: The Secret History of the FBI* (New York: St. Martin's Press, 2002), 124.
11.   Ibid.

12. Kathleen Cleaver, *Liberation, Imagination and the Black Panther Party: A New Look at Their Legacy* (New York: Routledge, 2001), 87.
13. Intelligence Activities and The Rights of Americans, Book One.
14. Freedom of Information and Privacy Acts, Fred Hampton, File #44-HQ-44202.
15. Ibid.

CHAPTER NINE—FIRED

1. "Accused Ford Assailant Reportedly Was Still a Federal Informer in the Days Before Gun Episode," *New York Times*, September 25, 1975, 29.
2. John Crewdson, "Moore Aided U.S. Firearms Unit Day Before Attack," *New York Times*, September 26, 1975, 1.
3. Sara Jane's recruitment story is taken from letters she wrote to me and from magazine and newspaper articles.
4. Andrew Hill, "Sara Jane Moore: Candid Conversation with the woman who tried to kill President Ford," *Playboy Magazine*, June 1976.
5. Personal interviews and letters with author and Sara Jane Moore, 1977–1978.
6. "All in the Family," *Time*, September 25, 1975.
7. Sara Jane told me in a conversation that she met Hearst at PIN and had been to a function at his home.
8. "Accused Ford Assailant," 29.
9. "Sally Moore FBI Informant," *Berkeley Barb*, July 20, 1975.

CHAPTER TEN—THE SPY

1. Photo of the United Prisoners Union Headquarters, Janet Fries, *The Berkeley Barb*, 1975.
2. "On the Job," *Berkeley Barb*, June 27, 1975.
3. Philip A. Klinker and Rogers M. Smith, *The Unsteady March: The Rise and Decline of Racial Equality in America* (Chicago: University of Chicago Press, 1999), 137.
4. "On the Job," *Berkeley Barb*, June 27, 1975.
5. Andrew Hill to author; *Playboy Magazine*, June 1976.

6. Vin McLellan and Paul Avery, *The Voices of Guns: The Definitive and Dramatic Story of the Twenty-two-month Career of the Symbionese Liberation Army* (New York: G. P. Putnam, 1976), 148.

7. Moore's letters to author.

8. Richard Vitamanti, FBI case agent, in interview with author, May 2003.

9. Ibid.

10. McLellan and Avery, *Voices of Guns*, 349–360.

11. Ibid., 356.

12. Ibid., 357. Moore's letters to author.

CHAPTER ELEVEN–THE MISSION

1. San Francisco News Bureau, "FBI Role In Popeye Mystery," *Berkeley Barb*, June 20, 1975, 5.

2. "Woman Led Tangled Life," *San Francisco Chronicle*, December 21, 1975.

3. Ibid., 3.

4. "FBI Role in Popeye Mystery."

5. Ibid.

6. John Irwin, *The Felon* (Engelwood Cliffs, NJ: Prentice-Hall, 1970), 208.

7. San Francisco History Project, Digital Library, "People's Food System," http://www.shapingsf.ctyme.com.

8. Marie Ferreboeuf, interview with author, March 20, 2008.

9. San Francisco History Project, Digital Library, "People's Food System."

10. Ibid.

11. Tom Buckley, "For Sara Moore, Brilliant Roles Enriched a Drab Life," *New York Times*, December 21, 1975, 4.

CHAPTER TWELVE–DOUBLING

1. Mark Bramhill, "On the Job," *Berkeley Barb*, June 27, 1975.

2. Ibid., 4.

3. Ibid.

4. Ibid.

5. Mark Bramhill, letter to editor, *Berkeley Barb*, July 4, 1975.

CHAPTER THIRTEEN—HUNTED

1. "Mystery Gunman Kills Two in S.F.," *San Francisco Chronicle*, June 9, 1975, 1.

2. Patty Singer, letter to the editor, *Berkeley Barb*, June 15, 1975.

3. United Prisoners Union, letter to the Editor, *Berkeley Barb*, June 20, 1975.

4. Ibid.

5. Venceremos, letter to the editor, *Berkeley Barb*, June 13, 1975.

6. Ibid.

7. San Francisco News Bureau, "FBI Role In Popeye Mystery," *Berkeley Barb*, June 20, 1975, 3.

8. Andrew Hill, "Sara Jane Moore: A Candid Conversation with the Woman Who Tried to Kill President Ford," *Playboy Magazine*, June 1976, 69–86.

9. Earl Satcher, letter to the editor, *Berkeley Barb*, August 8, 1975.

10. This interview was conducted in confidentiality, and the name of the interviewee is withheld by mutual agreement.

CHAPTER FOURTEEN—TESTING SECURITY

1. "Ford to Visit, Speak at World Affairs Council," *San Francisco Chronicle*, September 20, 1975, 1.

2. "Moore Aided Firearm's Unit Day Before Attack," *New York Times*, October 1, 1975, 1; "Protecting the President," *Time*, October 6, 1975, 12.

3. Ibid.

4. Ibid.

5. Ibid.

6. Ibid.

7. Ibid.

8. "Miss Moore Tried to Call Ford Guards Five Times," *New York Times*, October 1, 1975, 1–19.

9. "Accused Ford Assailant Reportedly Was Still a Federal Informer in the Days Before Gun Episode," *New York Times*, September 25, 1975, 29.

10. Moore to author, various correspondences, 1986.

11. "For Sara Moore, Brilliant Roles Enriched a Drab Life," *New York Times*, December 21, 1975.

12. "Protecting the President," *Time*, October 6, 1975, 12.

13. "Moore Worked in Federal Undercover Operation After Report of Threat Against Ford," *New York Times*, September 25, 1975, 29.

14. Ibid.

CHAPTER FIFTEEN—THE UNLIKELY ASSASSIN

1. "Can the Risk be Cut?" *Newsweek*, October 6, 1975.

2. "Ford Gun Bought in Danville," *San Francisco Chronicle*, September 24, 1975.

3. Ibid.

4. Richard Vitamanti, FBI case agent for *United States of America v. Sara Jane Moore*, stated in interview with Geri Spieler.

5. "Ford Gun Bought in Danville."

6. Carolyn Anspacher and Paul Avery, "Suspect's Story of Shooting," *San Francisco Chronicle*, September 23, 1975.

7. Ibid.

8. Carol Pogash, reporter for the *San Francisco Examiner*, in telephone interview with Geri Spieler, March 2005.

9. "Suspect's Story of Shooting."

10. Ibid.

11. "Driven By Frustration, Says Sara in Interview; Terms Security Stupid," *Charleston Daily Mail*, September 25, 1975.

12. President Gerald Ford, in telephone interview with Geri Spieler, December 12, 2003.

13. Tim Hettrich, who was on the scene in his role as a patrolman for crowd control, provided me with this account in an interview on October 10, 2008. This information is in contrast to reports in other documents I found, including the *New York Times*, *San Francisco Chronicle*, and other wire stories, which were not as detailed and did not include the personal point of view of Capt. Hettrich. Hettrich's concern was that if he could not keep Sara Jane's hand facing downward she could have shot him or someone else. He was equally concerned that if a fight broke out, her gun could become an out-of-control weapon. The

accounts of the event in the aforementioned news sources had only mentioned that Hettrich "*subdued*" Sara Jane.

CHAPTER SIXTEEN—"I ACTED ALONE"

1. *United States of America v. Sara Jane Moore*, 75–729 SC (U.S. District Court, Northern District of California), September 23, 1975, William Whittaker.
2. *United States of America v. Sara Jane Moore*, 75–729 SC (U.S. District Court, Northern District of California) October 6, 1975, William Whittaker.
3. *United States of America v. Sara Jane Moore*, 75–729 SC (U.S. District Court, Northern District of California), December 16, 1975, William Whittaker.
4. Carolyn Anspacher and Paul Avery, "Suspect's Story of Shooting," *San Francisco Chronicle*, September 23, 1975, p. 1.
5. Ibid.
6. *United States of America v. Sara Jane Moore*, CR 75–729 (U.S. District Court, Northern District of California) December 16, 1975, William Whittaker.
7. "Secret Service Warned About San Francisco Crowd," *Los Angeles Times*, September 25, 1975.
8. *United States of America v. Sara Jane Moore*, CR-75–729 SC (U.S. District Court, Northern District of California) October 28, 1975, William Whittaker.
9. Richard Vitamanti, in a conversation with Geri Spieler, March 2003.
10. Sara Jane Moore, CRF 75–729 SC, December 16, 1975.
11. Ibid.

CHAPTER SEVENTEEN—GUILTY

1. *United States of America v. Sara Jane Moore*, CR 75–729 (U.S. District Court, Northern District of California) October 6, 1979, William Whittaker; Sara Jane Moore, CR 75–729, November 17, 1975, Raymond Linkerman.
2. Medical records of the individual examinations of Sara Jane Moore are private and not available to the public. The available information

is from testimony at her sanity hearing, where several of the psychiatrists gave their conclusions for the public record, and is supplemented in testimony by her defense attorney, James Hewitt.

3. James Hewitt, interview, May 18, 2005.
4. Sara Jane Moore, CR 75–729, December 16, 1975, Raymond Linkerman.
5. James Hewitt, interview, May 18, 2005.
6. Sara Jane Moore, CR 75–729, December 12, 1975, William Whittaker.
7. Sara Jane Moore, CR 75–729, December 12, 1975, William Whittaker, Change of Plea.
8. Ibid.
9. Ibid.
10. Tom Buckley, "Judge Rules Miss Moore Is Competent to Change Plea to Guilty in Ford Shooting but Defers Acceptance," *New York Times*, December 16, 1975, 27.
11. Ibid.
12. Tom Buckley, "For Sara Jane Moore, Brilliant Roles Enriched a Drab Life," *New York Times*, December 21, 1975; and interviews conducted with several confidential sources.
13. Interviews were conducted by FBI informants who had been in the same radical community as Sara Jane. Members of the community were reluctant to implicate one of their own for fear of reprisals.

CHAPTER NINETEEN–THE PRISONER

1. *United States of America v. Sara Jane Moore*, CR 75–729 SC (U.S. District Court, Northern District of California) April 4, 1977, William Whittaker. Motion hearing to appeal sentence.
2. Sara Jane Moore, CR 75–729, April 15, 1977, William Whittaker. Motion filed to vacate sentence.
3. Sara Jane Moore, CR 75–729, May 16, 1977, William Whittaker. Martha Kirkpatrick, M.D., testifies on Sara Jane's state of mind.
4. Sara Jane Moore, CR 75–729, May 16, 1977, William Whittaker, Martha Kirkpatrick, M.D., testifies on Sara Jane's state of mind.
5. Ibid.
6. Ibid.

CHAPTER TWENTY—SETTLING IN AND BECOMING QUEEN

1. Janet refused to be interviewed about her mother.
2. Robin Toner, "Sara Moore Arraignment is Thursday," *Charleston Daily Mail*, February 8, 1979, 13A.
3. Ibid.
4. Rosalie Earle, "Jury to Study Martino Escape Case Today," *Charleston Gazette*, April 1979.
5. Ibid.
6. Ibid.
7. Robin Toner, "No Regret Charge 'Trash' Sara Jane Claims," *Charleston Gazetteer*, March 7, 1979, 1.

CHAPTER TWENTY-ONE—SOLITARY

1. I still store this art collection, as I had made a promise to Sara Jane to do so. I have tried to reach Frederic so that I could hand the art over to him, but he does not wish to be contacted. I have also offered it to her three other children, who have indicated that they do not want it. One of Sara Jane's siblings has indicated he might consider taking the pictures. I have no expectation of being paid for the costs of storing the works over these years, but I did explain to them that whoever takes the art will need to bear the costs of having them packaged for shipment, and shipped.

    In October 2008, Sara Jane contacted my publisher asking to arrange for her art collection to be retrieved from storage and returned to her. She provided no contact information but said that a representative of hers would be in touch to schedule the pickup. As this book goes to press, neither Sara Jane nor her representative has initiated any further contact.
2. "Ford Assailant Blocks Prison Key Crackdown," *San Francisco Chronicle*, August 2, 2000, A21.
3. Michael Taylor, "Sara Jane Moore, Who Tried to Kill Ford in '75, Freed on Parole," *San Francisco Chronicle*, January 1, 2008, http://www.sfgate.com/ (accessed April 6, 2008).

AFTERWORD

1. President Gerald Ford, in a telephone interview with Geri Spieler, December 12, 2003.

2. Ibid.

3. Charles R. Babcock, "Spy Agency Infighting Hurt U.S., Turner Says: Ex-CIA Director Critical of Rise in Covert Actions," *Washington Post*, May 13, 1985, p. A3.

4. United States Government Accountability Office testimony before the Committee on Government Reform, reported in the House of Representatives 9/11 Commission Report: *Reorganization, Transformation, and Information Sharing.* Issued August 3, 2004.

5. David Cook, "Reforming U.S. Intelligence," *Christian Science Monitor*, February 19, 2003.

6. Andrew Hill, "Sara Jane Moore: A Candid Conversation with the Woman Who Tried to Kill President Ford," *Playboy Magazine*, June 1976.

7. *United States of America v. Sara Jane Moore*, 75–729 SC (U.S. District Court, Northern District of California) October 6, 1975, William Whittaker.

BIBLIOGRAPHY

Bloom, Alexander and Wini Brienes. *Takin' It to the Streets: A Sixties Reader.* New York: Oxford University Press, 2003.

Brienes, Winnie. *Community and Organization in the New Left, 1962–1968: The Great Refusal.* Piscataway, NJ: Rutgers University Press, 1989.

Brook, James, Chris Carlsson, and Nancy Joyce Peters. *Reclaiming San Francisco: History, Politics, Culture.* San Francisco: City Lights Books, 1998.

Buhle, Paul. *History and the New Left Madison, Wisconsin, 1950–1970.* Philadelphia: Temple University Press, 1990.

Clarke, Gerald. "The Silent Generation Revisited," *Time* (June 1970).

Domhoff, William. "C. Wright Mills, Power Structure Research, and the Failures of Mainstream Political Science." *New Political Science* 29 (2007): 97–114.

Dutton, Frederick. *Changing Sources of Power: American Politics in the 1970s.* New York: McGraw-Hill, 1971.

Hill Andrew. "Sara Jane Moore: A Candid Conversation with the Woman Who Tried to Kill President Ford," *Playboy* (June 1976): 69–86.

Howe, Irving and Michael Harrington. *The Seventies: Problems and Proposals.* New York: Harper & Row, 1972.

Jackson, George. *Blood in My Eye.* New York: Random House, 1972.

Jackson, George. *Soledad Brother.* New York: Coward-McCann, 1970.

Kessler, Ronald. *The FBI: Inside the World's Most Powerful Law Enforcement Agency.* New York: Pocket Books, 1993.

Klinker, Philip A. *The Unsteady March: The Rise and Decline of Racial Equality in America.* Chicago: University of Chicago Press, 1999.

McLellan, Vin and Paul Avery. *The Voices of Guns: The Definitive and Dramatic Story of the Twenty-two-month Career of the Symbionese Liberation Army.* New York: Putnam, 1977.

Mills, C. Wright and Alan Wolfe, *The Power Elite*. New York: Oxford University Press, 2000.

Rafael, Tony. *The Mexican Mafia*. New York: Encounter Books, 2007.

Sands, Earl and Bennett Cohen. *Zebra Murders: A Season of Killing, Racial Madness, and Civil Rights*. New York: Arcade Publishing, 1997.

PERMISSIONS

INDEX